100 IDEAS
FOR SUPPORTING PUPILS WITH ADHD

ALSO AVAILABLE FROM CONTINUUM

100 IDEAS
FOR SUPPORTING PUPILS WITH ADHD

Geoff Kewley and Pauline Latham

B L O O M S B U R Y

LONDON • NEW DELHI • NEW YORK • SYDNEY

First published 2008 by Continuum International Publishing Group

Reprinted 2009, 2010, 2011, 2012, 2013, 2015, 2016, 2017
by Bloomsbury Education an imprint of Bloomsbury Publishing Plc
50 Bedford Square, London W1B 3DP

www.bloomsbury.com

ISBN: 978-0-8264-9660-7

© Geoff Kewley and Pauline Latham 2008

A CIP record for this publication is available from the British Library.

Designed and typeset by Ben Cracknell Studios | www.benstudios.co.uk
Printed and bound by CPI Group (UK) Ltd, Croydon, CR0 4YY

This book is produced using paper that is made from wood grown in
managed, sustainable forests. It is natural, renewable and recyclable.
The logging and manufacturing processes conform to the environmental
regulations of the country of origin.

CONTENTS

SECTION 3 **ADHD and the classroom**

SECTION 4 Behavioural difficulties

SECTION 5 Helping the pupil with organization

SECTION 6 Specific learning difficulties

SECTION 7 Handwriting problems

SECTION 8 Enhancing self-esteem and social skills

SECTION 9 Medication

SECTION 10 Gifted children with ADHD

SECTION 11 **Parents and colleagues**

SECTION 12 **Transitions**

SECTION 13 **ADHD with other difficulties**

INTRODUCTION

This book is a compilation of experience of the staff of
the Learning Assessment and Neurocare Centre (LANC)
in Horsham, West Sussex. The LANC has for many years
specialized in the assessment and management of
children with attention deficit hyperactivity disorder
(ADHD) and related neurodevelopmental difficulties.
The effective management of any child with ADHD,
and the ongoing monitoring of progress, require liaison
with the school, both before and after assessment, with
support in the introduction of specific educational
strategies.

For many teachers an appreciation of the concepts
of ADHD has helped them think differently about
common classroom problems of disruptive behaviour,
poor concentration and educational underachievement,
as well as dyslexia and dyspraxia. ADHD is now seen
as a valid condition and is a recognized disability.
A diagnosis of ADHD is not an excuse, rather an
explanation, for behaviours. It opens the door for
understanding the need for appropriate strategies and
accommodations to help a child achieve to his or her
potential, wherever this may be in the IQ range.

ADHD is a very important condition to special needs
and classroom teachers alike. The copious myths and
misinformation that have unfortunately surrounded the
condition in recent years have tended to obscure its
importance as a special educational needs condition.
Research clearly shows that ADHD is a condition of
brain dysfunction in which the neurotransmitters – the
chemical messengers of the brain – are not working
properly. This brain dysfunction leads to often significant
difficulties in the whole of life, not only in the
educational situation.

Children with ADHD can be extremely challenging
for teachers and can take up an inordinate amount of

time and emotional reserves. This book has been written to help you understand ADHD and therefore cope more effectively with these children and to implement the most evidenced-based strategies they need to guide them through their school years.

While both boys and girls do have ADHD, it is generally more common in boys. For convenience this book will refer to the child as 'him' or 'he' but the information and advice given could clearly also be relevant to girls.

In the compilation of this book, the authors would like to thank staff at LANC, including Zara Harris, Gillian Cameron, Nigel Humphrey, David Bracher, Rebecca Shaw, as well as Cathy Stead for the typing.

Preparing to teach the child with ADHD

ADHD is a complex condition seen in every classroom. As a teacher you can make life a lot more rewarding for yourself and these vulnerable pupils by gathering as much factual information about ADHD from as wide a range of informed sources as possible. Sharing this with colleagues, organizing and attending in-service training and conferences arranged by experienced professionals in the field can make all the difference to how effective your teaching and support for these children will be. The children will be able to enjoy the school experience much more and cope and flourish better if they are understood and cared for appropriately.

Symptoms of ADHD may be mild, moderate or severe or combined with other conditions such as specific learning difficulties or autistic spectrum problems, and maturity levels and skills in these pupils will vary depending on the severity and type of their symptoms and associated issues. Try to note down when and in what setting the child's difficulties are most problematic so that strategies can be tailored to support the child at these times.

ADHD is a biologically-based disability that gives rise to educational and behavioural difficulties. It is treatable, but not curable. You will need to be aware that interventions can have a powerful and positive impact, but that the refractory nature of ADHD means that many of these children will continue to experience difficulties in their academic and social lives, despite treatment.

Commonly, learning difficulties and other problems coexist with ADHD, especially academic, social and organizational problems. Such difficulties can include underachieving, being suspended or excluded, and rejection by peers. Understand that the goals of school intervention are to contain and manage the symptoms and to preclude or minimize the occurrence of secondary problems that are likely to happen to the child if the ADHD is not well managed.

ADHD is not due to a lack of skill or knowledge, but is a problem of sustaining attention, effort and motivation and of inhibiting behaviour in a consistent manner over time. This is especially true when consequences are delayed, weak or absent.

It is therefore essential to understand the basis of ADHD as you will be in a much better position to teach effectively and care for children with a wide range of difficulties. Try to:

o ascertain the profile of each child with ADHD in your class
o find out the child's strengths and weaknesses
o give more frequent and salient positive consequences for actions and behaviours, more consistent negative consequences and accommodations to assigned work
o acknowledge that it is harder for ADHD pupils to do the same academic work and exhibit the same social behaviour as would be expected of other pupils.

It is important that you think about your attitude to ADHD and try to evaluate what you know about the condition. Many teachers feel that unless a child is extremely hyperactive he does not have ADHD – is this your perspective?

Many teachers also find it hard to accept that the child just does not have the choice to concentrate. Reflect on what difference it might make to your handling of a child if he biologically has a difficulty in sitting still, can't help being verbally impulsive and calling out in class, and has short-term memory retention problems where he is more likely to forget homework or instructions. Does this alter the way in which you would teach, handle difficult situations and generally approach the child?

Reflect on the things that may have helped you in the past with children with these difficulties. Have you found that a firm approach, loose or clear boundaries, vague instructions or a certain teaching style make things better or worse? Is there any consistency?

Do you find it difficult to accept that these children have a medical condition and are not just wilfully naughty? Can you think of other ways, based on your previous experience with similar children, where changes of strategy may have been effective?

How do you feel if the child with ADHD is on medication? Do you understand the reasons why this might be done and what the aims of the medication are? Do you know the sort of symptoms that might be improved by medication and the sort of information that might be helpful for the medical profession to receive feedback on?

When you have read this book it might be a good idea to come back to these points and reflect on the knowledge you have acquired.

Aim to find out as much information as you can about ADHD through factual books, video presentations and websites. Talk to colleagues, obtain information packs and attend regular meetings and in-service training.

There is an enormous amount of information available online, but be careful to stay away from the websites that peddle misinformation. There are now a great many websites that provide information based on an international and ethical approach to ADHD, recognizing it as a valid disability.

One useful site is www.myadhd.com, a subscription-based website aiming to connect doctors, parents and teachers. It provides a large number of very appropriate rating scales and forms that can be electronically transmitted between professionals and parents. This means that teachers can receive and complete rating scales quickly and easily and the child's progress can be readily and jointly tracked. A great deal of other information is also available on this site regarding the management and treatment of children with ADHD, especially in relation to behaviour, socialization, study skills, anger management and organization.

Another website that is particularly useful for special needs educators is www.ldonline.org/ This site looks at all learning difficulties and has plenty of information related to ADHD in the overall educational setting.

Other useful websites include:

o www.lanc.uk.com
o www.help4adhd.org
o www.chadd.org
o www.addiss.co.uk
o www.adhdcarepathway.co.uk
o www.adders.org
o www.bullying.co.uk
o www.childline.org.uk
o www.kidscape.org.uk

A POSITIVE ETHOS

The overall school ethos is crucial to the success of managing a child with ADHD – often only slight changes of approach make a huge difference both to child and teacher. Your attitude to the child in front of his peers is very important. Have realistic expectations built on a good understanding of the facts about ADHD.

Children with ADHD will all be different from each other and therefore cannot all be treated in the same way. Try to cultivate understanding, support and respect between the children in the class and each member of the team, be they teachers, members of the medical profession, or other professionals. Here are some points to remember.

○ Be positive towards the child – don't ridicule him.
○ Find something the child does well and praise him in front of other children. Children tend not to befriend someone who is continually being criticized.
○ Build self-esteem by giving him a positive role – even if it is only being the goldfish monitor.
○ Act as a good role model, appreciating each child's strengths.
○ Always respect the child's confidentiality. Special arrangements for medication should not be common knowledge to the class. When medication is used, it should be seen as a way of allowing the child to be 'available' for good teaching and parenting strategies.
○ Build good relationships with parents, working with them constructively and keeping them regularly informed without condemning or preaching to them. A teacher's unprejudiced comments are vital for evaluation and monitoring of progress, especially before and after medical assessment.

So, take a moment to consider whether or not the overall school ethos is supportive of these children. Consider, too, whether there is cohesion among teachers and other members of staff in the management of these children. Discuss at staff meetings whether the systems are in place with regard to confidentiality and the various activities that children are involved in. Make sure other professionals are discreetly but adequately informed about the child's special educational needs. Discuss which particular activities might cause him more difficulties, and work together to find solutions – for example, having a buddy or a good role model to help support the child in small-group activities or on school trips.

Do not expect the child to become an angel overnight –
even when they are on medication there will still be
problems in some situations. This doesn't mean all is
lost, but it does require a philosophical approach and
understanding of the reality of ADHD which helps you
to get things into perspective – remember, children with
ADHD are not 'problem children' but 'children with a
genuine problem'.

Symptoms of ADHD present lifelong challenges.
ADHD is a potential life sentence. Some children –
approximately a third – may grow out of it, a third may
be able to manage their symptoms successfully as they
grow older, but a third will experience significant
symptomatic problems into adulthood.

Don't forget that the child with ADHD usually has
many positive qualities and skills that can be buried
underneath the struggles of suffering from ADHD –
the challenge is to discover and develop these to allow
the child to achieve to his potential and enjoy a better
quality of life.

Most of all, ensure that you have an up-to-date,
informed understanding of the facts and reality of
suffering from and living with ADHD and its appropriate
management so that you and your colleagues can
provide essential support to the child and each other.
It is important that everyone understands that this is a
neurological problem and empathizes appropriately with
the situation.

It is helpful to recognize that the symptoms and
signs of ADHD are different at different stages of
development, that medication is but one strategy in
helping these children – although frequently an essential
strategy – and that they will tend to have the symptoms
at least throughout their school life.

It is essential to develop a system – from the headteacher right through the school – to encourage a good understanding of ADHD.

This is a difficult thing to achieve and involves education. Often, such education initially appears to come from well-motivated and informed parents. However, teachers can find this sort of information from parents difficult to acknowledge or accept professionally. Thus, in-service training can be very useful if given by a professional who understands ADHD, its impact and the difficulties it creates for a child in the classroom, as well as for the teacher, so that these can be better understood and supported.

Because ADHD impacts not only on mainstream classroom teachers but also on the special educational needs coordinators (SENCOs), it is a good idea to make this a joint approach as part of the school's overall philosophy and as part of a special educational needs policy. Even having this information percolate through to lay staff, such as dinner ladies, giving them an understanding of how to approach children with ADHD in the unstructured lunchtimes can make such a difference.

Suggest that staff training be given to all members of the school about ADHD, identifying those children with ADHD and the sort of difficulties they experience. Detail any strategies that are already in place and why they are necessary for a particular child. Encourage support, rather than scepticism. Dispel myths about ADHD and emphasize that it should be recognized as a disability. It is critical that everyone is aware of the child's needs and follows a defined nurturing, rather than punitive, school policy in their dealings with the child. Offer to be a lead teacher in disseminating information about ADHD with school staff and monitoring the school's ethos in regard to these children.

Ask all staff to make directions and requests short, clear and direct. Make sure everyone understands that the child will need tasks and directions to be broken down into step-by-step activities. Social interactions need to be monitored and staff must be prepared to intervene before situations escalate.

Ask staff to set small and achievable tasks to give the child with ADHD focus and activity. For example, give the child prefect duties, set him fun 'challenges' such as running three laps around the playground, or encourage him to join a lunchtime activity or sports group to keep busy and engaged. Such activities can also help to boost self-esteem.

All children, but particularly those with ADHD who need good teaching to stimulate concentration, learn and respond better if the task is innovative, interactive, fun and motivating. Subtle changes of approach by you can make the difference between success and failure.

An engaging teaching style, empathy, a sense of humour and patience, a belief in the child and the teacher's ability to remain unflappable can make all the difference.

Always face the class and, initially, make eye contact. It is essential to keep instructions concise, brief and as clear as possible, giving one instruction at a time. Many children, especially those with ADHD, can be easily overwhelmed by too many instructions, and short-term memory problems may make this more difficult.

It helps these children if instructions are repeated, as well as having the rules written down. Making clear the consequences of not complying is also important. It is also a good idea to try to develop a private signal or cue for the child to start a task, or to help the child self-monitor if he is being too noisy.

Raise your expectations for their performance – but be realistic in this – and let them know what your expectations are. Let them know that you believe that they can succeed in your classroom, but that there will be a price to pay in terms of effort and organization. Let them know that you will help as much as possible.

MAKE TEACHING INTERESTING

Children with ADHD typically show wide variability in response to treatment and also quite marked day-to-day variability – more than most children. You should expect this variability and understand that the methods and programmes used one day may not work the next.

However, try to set boundaries and limits for the child, both in the classroom and playground. These should be clear, concise and constantly reinforced with limited choices. Make clear what is acceptable and what is not, so that the child knows exactly where he stands. It is important to have regular daily and weekly routines and to forewarn the child of any changes as children with ADHD do not react well to sudden changes of routine. The use of contracts, lists and reminders may also be helpful.

When methods fail that have worked previously, try not to attribute this to your inadequacies as a teacher, or think that the child is wilfully choosing to be like this. By recognizing that this is part of the child's disability, that it will happen no matter how excellent your management strategies, and riding out the difficult days, the good days will be more rewarding for both you and the child.

These children are being charged with a tremendous task – to sit still, pay attention and behave in a structured environment. With even the best teaching that is available, some children find it impossible to cope and they may eventually move into special needs provision. ADHD is often a lifetime disability but if you can teach these children as many new strategies, new habits and new coping techniques as possible, they have more chance of utilizing them and coping better in the future.

Remember, these children don't choose to be different but they are delayed in the process of developing these skills and/or have significant difficulty in applying them. Try not to be disheartened by the bad days. At the end of a bad day, try to convince yourself that there is a good chance tomorrow will be better, and remember the importance of acknowledging that it is the behaviour, not the child, that you find frustrating.

Because children with ADHD are easily distracted and easily bored, they benefit from having a fairly structured classroom setting, with, if possible, all seats facing the front, rather than an open plan classroom.

Try and seat the child with ADHD towards the front of the room in a position where distractions can be minimized and where he is close to the teacher. Seat the child as close as possible to you without giving the impression of being punitive. Also, sitting him close to another pupil who could be a good role model can help. If possible, increase the distance between the desks. Avoid seating the child at the back of the classroom or near hallways or windows, where he is likely to be distracted.

It is usually better to use rows in your seating arrangement and to avoid groups of pupils, which is often too distracting for the child with ADHD. Tables can be used for limited and specific group projects, and traditional rows for independent work. Sometimes a horseshoe shape works well.

Stand near the pupil with ADHD when giving directions or presenting the lesson. If appropriate, use the pupil's worksheet as an example when you are giving instructions, to show him exactly what you mean and help him to stay focused.

Educational strategies for children with ADHD are largely general, good teaching strategies that benefit all children in the classroom. However, for the child with ADHD they are particularly necessary.

Have a well-established daily routine in the classroom and a clear system for keeping track of what work has been done and what has yet to be finished. These children need structure, routine and predictability.

Set a good example by having a well-organized classroom which is tidy and calm and yet well structured. This will encourage the children to organize their desks and their time on a regular basis but they will need to be taught how to go about it. Typically, children with ADHD have extremely poor organizational skills and time management as they have a very poor concept of time passing.

If possible, have a quiet area that is available for all children but can be used when there are upsets in the classroom and the child needs somewhere to go to calm down.

Have good visual clues on the blackboard or whiteboard, with a clear plan for when various assignments are due.

If you have to seat your pupil with ADHD at a table, leave an empty seat next to him. This will allow for a bit more wriggle room and also provide a seat for you to slip into easily to offer added assistance or to direct focus.

Allow for alternative seating – this can be used for all pupils at different times but can be useful to allow movement for the child with ADHD. This extra seating might be a standing desk, a desk with a ball chair (a chair made from a frame that supports a large therapy ball), a kneeling desk, or even a lying down desk. Having a regular alternative seat in a different area of the room can provide a necessary break for the fidgety pupil with ADHD.

All children have different learning styles, as do teachers. It is helpful to analyse your own learning style as a teacher to better understand the way you might come across. This can help you become better equipped to teach all kinds of children, especially those who struggle with conditions such as ADHD. So, ask yourself, what kind of learner are you?

o Visual – learns through pictures, videos, etc.
o Auditory – learns by listening
o Kinaesthetic – learns through active involvement and experience
o Tactile – learns by building models and making things.

It is said that about a third of pupils do not process auditory information well, that about two-thirds perform better with tactile and kinaesthetic learning, and about half of pupils have some difficulty with organization and processing of information.

While all children's learning styles need to be ascertained, children with ADHD tend not to be particularly good auditory learners. They are likely to benefit from maps, graphs, pictures, diagrams and writing with coloured markers and chalk. They tend to be global learners and may need to see the whole picture before making sense of the individual components.

Their learning style may mean experimenting with classroom seating arrangements, especially in junior school, ascertaining whether a semi-circle, a table cluster, or staggered arrangement of desks works best for the child.

Ask the child what environment he thinks he works best in. Is he better in a classroom that is well lit, where he is sitting by the window, when the room is hot rather than cold, or when there is more or less activity? Is he better doing projects alone or working with others? Does he prefer to have headphones – working with or without music? Ask him to describe his perfect classroom. You can use this information in helping to develop better management and classroom strategies.

Lesson time

Always begin the lesson with a simple overview of what you want the pupils to achieve. Then create a framework with simple steps so the child with ADHD knows what is meant to happen next. Developing a sequence of events is helpful as many of these children have organizational difficulties and benefit from clear sequencing and structure. This can encourage them to start to take responsibility for their own learning and behaviour. As a result their self-esteem is improved and they will hopefully demand less of your time.

You will need to ensure that the pupil is as prepared as possible for the lesson:

o Create a routine for starting any activity – the same words, a song, a bell, a clap.

o Make sure that the pupil has all the books and supplies necessary before starting (provide duplicate sets if necessary).

o Make sure that the pupil has had a stretch break before starting an assignment.

o Provide direct supervision as the pupil starts and completes the first sentence/problem.

o Provide prompts to help him get going – for example, write a question that requires an answer, such as when writing a biography, 'When was he born?' 'Where was he born?'

o Provide an outline rather than a blank piece of paper when starting work.

o Teach the pupil to make his own outline so that he knows exactly what to put on the empty page before he has to think 'what to write'.

o Use software such as *Kidspiration* or *Inspiration* to provide an outline that prompts the pupil to start writing.

If you are working with teenagers, try to include the pupil as a partner in the planning and problem-solving process – i.e. going beyond simply manipulating and controlling the pupil's behaviour. This may mean giving more support for longer than their peers. Don't expect miracles!

In this lesson:

1. L.O.

2.

3.

4.

Transition music + IWB pics:

maths

sharp!

It is a good idea to provide an outline of the lesson, with key concepts and vocabulary, prior to the more detailed presentation. This helps pupils to follow and understand the main concepts and terms as the lesson unfolds. Telling your pupils why and what they are learning is important and helps to keep them motivated.

Pupils with ADHD often benefit from being assigned to a group with a specific role or piece of information that must be shared. Using cooperative learning techniques can be useful, as can pairing pupils to check work. Also, using other pupils to act as tutors for the child with ADHD can be very helpful.

All children, but particularly those with ADHD, respond to a variety of learning activities during each lesson. Multi-sensory presentations, including audio-visual aids if they are not too distracting, help to ensure that interesting pictures and sounds relate directly to the material that is being taught.

It can help to make modifications to the curriculum, such as abbreviating assignments, increasing work time, reducing the number of problems per page, or using worksheets rather than books.

Use computers as much as possible with children with ADHD as they are excellent for providing immediate feedback and a multi-sensory approach, preventing the child from becoming bored. *PowerPoint* or *Astound* presentations can also be very effective.

Pupils with ADHD can really benefit from well-designed worksheets. Keep the page format simple, using large type, and make important points easy for the pupil to find. Avoid the use of extraneous pictures or visual elements that are unrelated to the issue. For some pupils using buff coloured paper rather than white is helpful if the room's lighting creates a glare. Write clear, simple directions and underline key direction words or vocabulary or have the pupils underline these words as you read directions with them. Put borders around parts of the page you want to emphasize so that their attention is drawn to these.

'Usability' is essential. Just as web designers strive to make websites fast, easy to navigate, and more user friendly, you should strive to make your worksheets easy to understand, easy to navigate and user friendly.

A simple method for making worksheets more manageable for pupils with ADHD is to photocopy the same worksheet (on A4 paper) onto A2 size paper, essentially doubling the size of everything. Poorly photocopied sheets should be avoided as this adds more distraction on the page. Highlighting relevant portions of the worksheet may be useful, such as where the pupil is supposed to fill in the gaps.

Because pupils with ADHD are often overwhelmed by too much information on a page, having more pages but with less on each page can be a solution. Providing more white space around each question allows them to focus better. Also, providing more writing space for the ADHD pupil with handwriting problems is often necessary – sometimes the same worksheet with double spacing will provide the space needed, or it may be necessary to simply place more space between questions.

Because pupils with ADHD have poor concentration, poor time management and are disorganized and frequently anxious, they often underachieve relative to ability and do poorly on long or timed tests, even when they know the material. They may benefit from tests with modified structure and being allowed extra time for examinations.

Try providing the pupil with a window pane card (a piece of card with a hole cut in it the size of one question) so that he can focus on one question at a time. Or prepare a test paper with plenty of white space around each question, thereby limiting the visual distractions on the page. Give plenty of opportunities to practise tests, and do short quizzes to help pupils prepare for the real thing.

A useful piece of software to help with examination practice is *Kurzweil* (www.kurzweiledu.com), initially designed for people with visual problems but now being widely used in schools for children with dyslexia. Examination papers or passages from a textbook can be scanned onto the computer (or downloaded from the internet), and the computer then 'reads it aloud' through speakers or headphones. It highlights the words as they are read and can be adjusted to suit the speed and needs of the reader.

Read the test aloud.

Consider seeking approval for modifying the test environment for pupils with ADHD. Being able to take a test in a quiet environment with few distractions will frequently enable the pupil to perform more to his ability. Where there are associated problems with handwriting and memory, obtaining permission for the pupil to use a tape recorder, to record test answers and assignments, or to have oral examinations, can be appropriate accommodations. The child's confidentiality should be respected, and any special arrangements for medication or modification of expected class standards of achievement should not be made common knowledge. Think of ways to discreetly deal with those issues without drawing attention to the pupil.

Children with ADHD are able to concentrate, keep on task and inhibit inappropriate behaviours much better when using computers. They usually respond well to computer-based tasks, especially when there is instant feedback from the interaction and colourful animations.

It is a good idea to ascertain how quickly any child with ADHD can type, and how interested they are in using computers. Some children are not interested and others are good at typing and prepared to use a computer for essays and longer work, but not for classroom situations.

Try presenting tasks in a computerized format – as a Word document rather than a pen and paper task – as children with ADHD will be able to take in more information. Documented instructions or information on the computer can be referred back to as often as the child needs, thus reducing the demands on the child's memory. Research suggests that using a computerized format, linked with interactive cartoon characters can help increase a child's engagement with a task and reduce fidgety, out-of-seat behaviour. The computer can also provide non-judgemental feedback which doesn't have the complications of face-to-face feedback. With this in mind, consider giving feedback via email or a Word document or online forum.

For older pupils, using computers to help with coursework can result in much more effective work being done. Show them how to use *PowerPoint* software to make study cards and to do revision work, as it makes the tasks more interesting. Including colour andanimations can turn it into a multi-sensory learning experience. Also, teach the pupils to use the 'label' programme on *Word* in order to print labels that can be stuck onto cards for revision work. If you are revising vocabulary, put the word in one colour and the definition in another so that it makes the cards easier to sort.

There is a wide range of computerized educational software available which can be particularly motivating and engaging for children with ADHD, so why not have a look at what's on offer? A good place to start is Sherston Software Limited, www.sherston.com/

Although children with ADHD usually have weak concentration, many are in fact able to focus – or even over-focus – on tasks they find particularly interesting. It is important not to fall into the trap of thinking that because they are often able to focus well on tasks they find interesting, if they tried harder they should be able to concentrate on the more mundane tasks. Children with ADHD find it very difficult indeed to do this.

With younger children especially, interspersing academic work with periods of exercise can be helpful. Give the child reasons to move around, perhaps to take a message or help with something in the classroom.

One-to-one tuition/small class size is particularly helpful if it is possible. Try to have frequent eye contact with the child with ADHD who might be daydreaming, and keep the task as interesting and stimulating as possible. Directions need to be given one step at a time. When a series of instructions is given, retention beyond the first direction is difficult. Minor adjustments on the part of the teacher in giving directions will help the pupil a great deal.

Try to catch your ADHD pupils being on task, and reward them. A reward as simple as a smile, nod, or a positive comment can go a long way. This tends to result in an actual increase in their attention span and time on task.

When the ADHD pupil is off task, either ignore him or redirect him back to his work, depending on the situation. As soon as he is back on task, reward his on-task behaviour with a smile, comment, pat on the back, and so on.

Because these pupils have difficulty with sustaining attention on tasks over time, they get bored very easily, even by you. The pupil will respond better to situations that he finds stimulating and engaging. Varying the instructional medium and pace will help sustain his interest. For example, it is usually helpful to break the task into small interesting segments. Try and alternate between high and low interest tasks. Teach as much academic work as possible in the morning when the child

KEEPING THE CHILD ON TASK

is most likely to be concentrating. Give short-term, immediate rewards to keep him motivated.

Many pupils with ADHD find lessons that emphasize hands-on activities highly engaging. Try to keep the time required for sustained attention to a task balanced with more active learning as this will improve your attention deficit pupil's performance. Changes in your voice level and variation in pace will also increase his attention during instruction.

Break long tasks into a series of shorter 'sprints' – the same amount of work, just organized differently so that he can work with focus, rest for a few seconds and see how he did, then work again. Combine your verbal directions along with illustrations or demonstrations of what you want your pupils to do. The more ways you use to describe what you want your ADHD pupils to do, the greater the likelihood that they will actually do it.

Sometimes it helps to ask the pupil with ADHD how long he thinks it would take to perform a certain task. Let him set his own time and work against a timer to try to provide more structure and hopefully some concept of the time it takes to do specific tasks.

Stressing accuracy instead of quantity of work can be important, so that mastery of a subject can be achieved.

Mistakes should be used to demonstrate more positive ways for future learning (rather than concentrating on the failure by discussing why and how things went wrong). Talk about what the child did positively and how things might be improved in the future. Remember, children with ADHD are used to experiencing failure in many aspects of their lives.

The medications used to treat ADHD vary in timing and effect. If you find concentration is very good at one time of the day and not at another time, it is a good idea to let the parents or child's physician know about these difficulties so that appropriate medication dosage adjustments can be considered. If possible, it is best to schedule the most attention-demanding tasks for the ADHD pupil during this medication window (see Section 9 for more on medication).

STAYING FOCUSED IN CLASS

Hyperactive pupils' bodies are driven to move constantly and it might be said that you can either have them sitting still or paying attention, but to do both is asking too much. For these pupils the trick is to find something that allows them to move without distracting you, other pupils or indeed themselves too much.

A box of acceptable fidget toys kept on your desk that can readily be supplied to any pupil in need of a 'fidget' is often useful. There should be classroom rules about how the fidget toy may or may not be used and it should be returned to the box at the end of the lesson so that another can be used at a later date – novelty of the fidget toy is often important and what works one day may not the second, so an ever-changing creative collection is needed.

A fidget box might include:

o A variety of squishy toys
o Koosh Balls
o Different types of fabric – ribbons are useful (velvety, shiny, springy etc.)
o Interesting erasers and pencil sharpeners
o Interesting pens and pencils
o Small toys which move without sound
o Pieces of Blu-Tack – or similar putty.

Allow acceptable movement. Have a stretch break for all the pupils and get them to do ten chair push-ups, or touch their toes ten times. Make the pupils with ADHD responsible for handing out papers, sharpening pencils or opening the door for visitors.

Placing a rubber, inflated (Move 'n' Sit) cushion (see www.backinaction.co.uk/move-n-sit) on the child's chair requires the pelvic and trunk muscles to constantly adjust in order to keep the body upright. These movements are often sufficient to satisfy the body's need to move, allowing the pupil to focus better on seated tasks. A cheaper option is to use a beach ball partially inflated and placed on a chair – this can have the same effect but will need to be replaced more frequently.

Other chairs that allow for movement such as office chairs, rocking chairs and ball chairs (a chair made from a frame that supports a large therapy ball) can be used to contain the movement in a more acceptable way and are safer than having the child constantly rocking on the back legs of a classroom chair.

If these strategies do not work, putting something in their mouths can. For some people chewing gum works wonders and can help focus the mind! While this may not be allowed in many schools, it can be quite an effective strategy. Two pieces of gum require extra chewing and provide more intense stimulation to the receptors in the jaw. Pupils will often chew things, shirt sleeves, collars, finger nails, pencils, so finding something acceptable to chew on can be important. Plastic therapy tubing is sometimes used to make a necklace that can be chewed.

INCREASING ALERTNESS: TASTE, TOUCH AND MOVEMENT

For the pupil who cannot get his head off the desk or the hyperactive pupil who cannot seem to calm down, you need to learn ways to stimulate levels of alertness.

Discovering each person's 'sensory diet' is useful. This technique involves working out how to use the sensory system to alter levels of alertness. For example, a strong peppermint or a sour boiled sweet may be used to wake up the taste buds which will in turn wake up the nervous system and get the head off the desk. Everybody's sensory system is different and so it is necessary to find out what works for each person. Here are some suggestions:

Taste. Put something in your mouth:
o Sour: pickles, gherkins, sour sweets
o Sweet: fruit, sweets (sugarless if preferred)
o Spicy: salsa, beef jerky
o Crunchy: nuts, carrots, pretzels, apples
o Chewy: gum, raisins, bagels, cheese
o Licking: boiled sweets, lollipops
o Sucking: drinking through a straw
o Biting: liquorice, toffee.

Movement (at least every hour):
o Isometrics – push-ups on wall or chair
o Aerobics or a brisk walk, run an errand
o Run up and down steps
o Shake head quickly
o Roll neck slowly in a circular motion
o Use a rocking chair or ball chair
o Do Theraband exercises (Theraband is a wide elastic band used to add resistance in exercise programmes such as pilates or in physiotherapy)
o Use timer/computer alarm as a reminder of when to stop work and stretch or move.

Touch:
o Fidgets – Koosh Ball, stress ball, rubber bands, etc.
o Rub gently or vigorously on skin or clothing

- Change temperature – open window, move fan
- Wash face with hot or cold face flannel
- Pet an animal
- Stroke a piece of velvet or satin
- Hold or lean up against a stuffed animal/pillow
- Deep pressure – many fidgety pupils like the feeling of something heavy on their lap or around their neck. Weighted cushions can be purchased for this purpose or simply made using a few pounds of rice as a filling. A long thin one can be placed on the shoulders of a pupil and a shorter fat one for the lap.

Use some of these ideas to stimulate alertness in your ADHD pupil.

Sight (changing the visual environment can be alerting/calming):

o Put on bright/dim light
o Look out of a window and focus on the horizon
o Clear the desk or table if clutter distracts the pupil
o Watch fish in an aquarium
o Look at a picture/photo of a peaceful scene
o If on a computer – look at a book/magazine.

Sound: Allow the use of earphones either with no music in order to shut out distracting noise in the environment or to add sound that acts as white sound to the pupil, blocking out distracting sounds. White sound will be different for each pupil and they will have to experiment to find what works for them. Sound can also be used to alter states of alertness and this too will need experimentation. Examples to try include:

o Music – even, slow beat
o Music – loud bass, uneven beat
o TV or radio
o Sing-along music
o Special CDs are now available with 'relaxation' or 'alerting' mixes
o Use different types of earphones – choose carefully
o White sound recordings of fountains, waves on the beach, streams, etc.

Smell: Caution should be employed when using smells as some smells may have powerful effects on the nervous system of your pupil or others seated nearby. However, some smells are very alerting, such as smelling salts and ammonia, while others are calming, such as lavender. Markers and pencils now come with smells! Experiment with what works best for each pupil – many pupils with ADHD are hypersensitive to smell and it may actually be necessary to remove the source of a smell.

ADHD and the classroom

Make an effort to find out about potential problems before a child enters your class by checking through previous reports, discussing him with previous teachers and finding out which strategies worked best in different situations. Find out whether he has difficulty coping with change or waiting his turn, if he tends to call out in class or needs to be cued in frequently in order to concentrate. Once the potential difficulties have been ascertained, think about how these difficulties will impact on the normal school day and on different situations that might arise. By doing this, you can plan ahead to avoid the possibility of a poor start. If you are fully informed, you will be able to prevent him letting himself down. Always try to play to the child's strengths, whatever they may be, and try to see more positives than negatives.

Discussing with informed colleagues the difficulties you are having in coping with a particular child can be a constructive step towards improving the relationship with that child. It is also a good idea to provide evidence of, and record, behavioural difficulties so that you have a clear record and can perhaps avoid future incidents.

Try to work towards upholding classroom or group rules to cultivate understanding and support and to avoid being asked why the difficult child is being allowed to do something when the other children are not. If you can do this, the other children are more likely to accept the difficult child (rather than reject or react to him) and you are more likely to learn to extinguish unwanted behaviour by ignoring it and paying attention to others who are behaving well.

Don't exclude the child from an event, but provide an alternative, with other children joining in, to avoid ostracism. For example, if a child has poor coordination and cannot take part in sports days, giving him a responsible job such as a door or drink monitor, or collating the results is a good idea. Try to make it a position where other children need to interact with him, so he can be made to feel special.

Although ADHD is much more common in boys, girls can also suffer from it and the condition is almost certainly under-recognized.

There are some subtle but significant differences in ADHD between boys and girls. Although girls are often not hyperactive, when they are they tend to be more fidgety and less motor-driven than boys, and to be more verbally and emotionally impulsive than physically impulsive. However, occasionally girls can be extremely motor-driven and, if not channelled correctly, can have major difficulties.

They may have difficulties in other, slightly tangential, ways and because they are not hyperactive they just 'fade away' in class and underachieve. Watch out for the girls in your class who:

o have very low and often intractable self-esteem
o are quite depressed and anxious
o sometimes self-harm
o lack confidence in social interactions.

It is all too easy to put this down to being 'just the way the child is'. However, try to watch the pupil carefully and note whether or not she is daydreaming and tends to be unaware of what is happening. In particular, think about whether or not she can be quite bright and whether her brightness may be enabling her to mask the fact that she is switched off for quite a lot of the class time.

Be aware that although this pupil will not be causing you so much difficulty with disruptive behaviour, calling out in class, and so on, her difficulties may be just as important.

Older teenagers with ADHD are more prone to emotionally impulsive comments and to spending impulsively. They can be easily led, drink and smoke excessively and have a much higher incidence of teenage pregnancy. Remember, girls may be adversely affected by changes in the menstrual cycle and their difficulties may be more pronounced at some times of the month than at others.

GIVING INSTRUCTIONS

A child with ADHD will benefit from being taught to follow instructions, to think before acting and to become aware of the consequences of his actions. Strategies such as '1,2,3' or 'Stop, Think, Do' are essential (see the book *1,2,3 Magic* by T. Phelan).

Aim to act immediately to intervene if the behaviour is inappropriate, to prevent it becoming out of control. On the count of 'One' the instruction is given, on 'Two' it is reinforced, and by the count of 'Three' the child must have complied, otherwise pre-agreed consequences come into play. By doing this it is usually possible to move on quickly to a more positive area. Avoid disciplining a child by withdrawing activities that he does well. Try to use penalties that do not damage his self-esteem or give him little chance to repair the misdemeanour.

These strategies are particularly useful with young children, as they aim to provide a very clear structure with immediate consequences that strongly counteract the child with ADHD's tendency to push boundaries and act impulsively. Using immediate positive feedback or punishment gives the child very clear boundaries. They can be modified to operate in a wide range of situations, such as the supermarket or at dinner with friends, as well as at school.

Positive instructions such as, 'Put your feet on the floor' rather than, 'Don't put your feet on the desk' will have more effect. Make it clear that it is the behaviour that is unacceptable, not the child. Don't give instructions until the class is quiet and everyone is listening. Many children with ADHD have problems with auditory instructions and, if dyslexic, may also have problems with visual instructions. Therefore, write the key points down as well as discussing them. Check that the instructions or topic have been understood, correct the pupil's mistakes immediately, and give him immediate positive feedback.

When you have a difficult situation with your ADHD pupil, try to consider what factors have initiated the particular behaviour and/or maintained it, and whether there are any wider issues, such as problems at home, bullying, learning difficulties, poor social skills, that you could help with. By doing this, you can better understand the behaviours, antecedents and consequences and help the child develop behaviours that lead to academic and social success.

Consider what strengths the pupil has for you to work with, as most people with ADHD have some activities where their impairments are absent – especially those activities they are particularly interested in. Note those activities where the signs of ADHD may be minimal or absent – such as when the pupil is under very strict control, is in a novel setting, is engaged in especially interesting activities, in a one-to-one situation or a situation where he experiences frequent rewards for appropriate behaviour. Try and build on these by gradually introducing slightly more difficult challenges, while continuing the structure in the situation. Children with ADHD rarely display the same level of dysfunction in all settings at all times, largely because of the degree of interest and different responses to different environments.

Try to approach the problems proactively – before they happen – rather than reactively – after they happen. Children with ADHD are often unable to acquit themselves when questioned, readily resorting to the most transparent excuses or lying, not covering up their tracks and often not seeming to know why they did a thing or denying having done it, even when witnessed. The approach you take to such a problem will very much influence the intervention and the outcome for the child.

These children also are often extremely hypersensitive to words, actions and situations. They often overreact to apparently minor – to the observer – triggers. They can also misinterpret. Bear this in mind when talking to them.

THINKING BEYOND THE IMMEDIATE PROBLEM

Try keeping a collaborative profile to reflect the pupil's academic skills in addition to personal interests, qualities and achievements. It is important that an equal number of positives and negatives are presented in a sensitive manner.

For each difficulty it is critical that a method or strategy is outlined to help overcome the problem. Focus on the differences in strengths and difficulties across contexts and at different times of the day. For example:

o I can concentrate better after sports class.
o I can pay attention for a lot longer if I'm an active participant or I'm really motivated.
o I get really distracted when I am hungry.
o I work better on the computer.

If possible develop a 'Signs that I need help' and 'Action plan' component to the profile.

There are many ways the profiles can be presented to make them more engaging and pupil-centred. You might consider using typewritten booklets and photo diaries. Imaginative ideas like this can provide the basis for negotiations about particular 'contracts' that can be drawn up to help identify specific boundaries and desired behaviour from both parties (see Idea 43).

Try specifying with the pupil what needs to be negotiated to ensure that 'contracts' are not broken, and emphasize that the pupil's views are equally as important as those of the staff. Identify a safe and secure place for the storage of the profile in order to maintain confidentiality and to minimize the chances of the document being lost or damaged. It is beneficial for a range of different people to have input into the profile, but this should be done in consultation with the pupil.

RULES

Aim to have as few rules as is necessary in the classroom. Make sure they are visible and the child knows them and is clear about the consequences of compliance or non-compliance. Rules should be phrased clearly and positively, for example: 'Be kind to others and listen when the teacher is speaking.' Don't make them too long. Praise and reward appropriate behaviour and achievements – try to ignore minor bad behaviour. Set boundaries for the child in the classroom and playground.

The child with ADHD may need help in appreciating rules and procedures in the classroom and find them hard to remember. Enforce rules consistently and quickly – children with ADHD cannot await rewards and will forget why they are punished if there is a delay. They don't like the rules to change.

Recognize that 'being fair' might not necessarily require that all children are treated identically. Rules and expectations may need to be individualized, but should be applied fairly and consistently. This does not mean that children with ADHD should not be accountable for their actions; you will also have other children in the class who have special needs and require specific support. They should have to comply with the rules, which have been tailored to their needs, and be able to achieve what is expected of them. The threat of punishment actually has very little influence on deterring the child with ADHD from breaking the rule, since his understanding of cause and effect is poor.

REWARDS AND PUNISHMENTS

Try to use reward systems that give the child opportunities to be rewarded frequently. Reinforcement and meaningful rewards are more effective than punishment, as is a positive attitude, comment or smile. It is usually necessary to change the reinforcers frequently as the child can become bored very quickly. Have significant immediate consequences for both encouraging and motivating the child as well as delivering sanctions.

It is important to bear in mind that if you make the punishment too extreme, the child may give up trying to behave well. You need to punish carefully – the punishment must be matched to the misdemeanour and you should work on one difficult behaviour at a time. Remember, you are teaching the child to behave just as you teach him to read.

It is also important to remember, even in difficult situations, that the child with ADHD has an underlying disability and that he is more vulnerable to these difficulties. Make sure the child understands it is his choice whether to be rewarded or punished. Don't assume that he will necessarily behave well because there is a reward.

Whenever possible, try to give the child with ADHD an opportunity to be responsible – don't resent doing so because he doesn't deserve it – and remember to think of him as having a type of disability. Provide opportunities for him to do a job or run an errand so that he can be allowed to retreat without losing face if he has become very upset or stressed.

It can also be helpful to try also to give the child a second chance to succeed as soon as he has failed, i.e. 'As soon as you say you are ready to be quiet you can leave the naughty chair/return to the room.'

Teach the child problem-solving skills so that he feels in control and hopefully when things go wrong next time he will handle the situation more effectively.

Home-based reward programmes can be very effective and are worth trialling with your ADHD pupil. For this you need good communication between teachers and parents. The teacher sends home a pre-agreed evaluation on the child's academic and behavioural progress at the end of each day. This daily school behaviour report card can be individualized with the child's name and date of birth at the top, the behaviours or goals that are being targeted listed on the left-hand side and the performance grades from 1 (excellent) to 5 (very poor) listed across the card. The teacher then rates the behaviours or goals during the day, putting a tick in the appropriate box, and the card is sent home daily. Short-term tokens on a daily basis can then be given by the parents, with longer-term rewards at the end of each week or fortnight. Homework can also be included in this.

It is best to target only a couple of behaviours or goals at a time, and focus initially on the main behaviours that need improvement or changing. Try to include positive as well as negative things so the child has the opportunity to earn points early on in the programme. The behaviours targeted may include a combination of academic, social and behavioural targets. They must be individualized depending on the problems. It might be, for example, staying in his seat, following directions, completing tasks, playing well with others or reducing aggression.

If the programme is to be successful there must be a clear and regular way for the teacher's reports to be translated into consequences at home. Sometimes it is helpful for the rewards at home to be combined with classroom-based programmes, extra activities or rewards.

Children with ADHD tend to need stronger and more powerful rewards and therefore those available through the home setting can often be more effective.

HOME-BASED REWARD PROGRAMMES

UNDERSTANDING CONSEQUENCES

Children with ADHD need far more immediate and salient consequences than other pupils. Instead of reprimanding them, use consequences in their management – use positives before negatives. Instead of first thinking of a punishment when you have a problem with a child, use incentives to develop the positive behaviours you want to encourage, i.e. teach them to stop and then to monitor situations, giving them an opportunity to repair situations, work better next time and to decide what is most important. For example, if there has been a fracas in the playground and a fight has developed, the ADHD child may have reacted impulsively. Discussing the outcome with him, talking through how this might have been prevented and acting out a scenario for the future can be helpful.

The child with ADHD is less likely to learn through experience, since the new and unfamiliar tend not to be readily assimilated. Differentiate between low *ability* and low *attainment*. For example, quite bright children can be significantly underachieving because of their difficulties with concentration. It is useful to be conscious of the fact that, because of their difficulties, their attainment – even with the most skilled teaching – remains below their chronological age. In this situation it may be that they have missed out on so much schoolwork before the treatment of their ADHD that they still have a lot of catching up to do. It may be that their problems with concentration remain and their medical treatment needs adjustment, or it may be that there is a need for further fine-tuned educational strategies or that there is the possibility of an associated specific learning difficulty.

Pupils who are disruptive are more likely to be removed from the classroom if their behaviour affects the other children. However, such actions may have a serious effect on the amount of academic material covered by the child, and if possible steps should be taken to minimize these removals.

Poor behaviour may also be used as an 'escape' mechanism by a pupil, particularly where tasks are difficult or he is worried about failure, so a detention will often be a positive reward for a child who aims to avoid a task or demand. By giving a detention you may unwittingly be reinforcing bad behaviour.

Detentions can also be counterproductive as, not only is the child with ADHD likely to forget to attend, he is often unable to concentrate sufficiently at the end of the school day. Detentions can also lead to poor staff and pupil relationships and will impact negatively on the child's self-esteem.

Try considering alternatives to detentions where possible. For example, you could use a token economy system where there are a number of tokens or chips, each of which has a value and which are given on a daily basis in a positive way to reinforce desired behaviour and taken away if a negative behaviour occurs.

Try and ignore negative behaviours where possible when they are minimal. Try distracting as a means of re-engaging the child's focus. Consider asking him to move to a different place in the class, break up long activities with short physical exercises, allow very brief time-out sessions (a few minutes), and use non-verbal feedback cards or prompts to let the child know he needs to adjust his behaviour and to prompt on-task focus. If and when detention is required, try to use it as a last resort and schedule a session in the timetable for the pupil to recap on material missed.

ALTERNATIVES TO DETENTION

Unstructured times such as breaktimes and lunchtime can often be a particular challenge to the pupil with ADHD because he has to organize his behaviour in the absence of structure and negotiate subtle social interactions. Try to use these times constructively – they are important to the pupil's social and personal welfare.

Prepare the child with ADHD for changes in routine so that he is not caught off guard. If problems persistently occur in the unstructured times, talk them through with the pupil and try to prevent recurrence.

Try giving him a particular role or rewarding activity during these times, to use computers or gain additional support in a subject where he is struggling, but ensure that he receives an adequate break and social time to avoid the perception that such measures are punitive or discriminatory. Try using this time as an alternative to doing homework out of school – a particularly positive incentive for some pupils.

Having a 'lunch buddy' can be good idea, especially if this is a slightly older child who may have similar interests. Use warning signals to indicate that the breaktime is coming to an end. Lunchtime activities may have to be restructured so that the child with ADHD does not have to wait to take turns or enter games. It is vital that other staff members or classroom helpers monitoring the lunch break are made aware of the child's specific difficulties.

Using a behaviour report card that links home and school is another useful strategy. This is similar to the home–school report card but the targets are issues that are more related to free time, such as not pushing, not teasing or taunting others, getting on with other children and not being involved in fighting.

A child with ADHD experiencing difficulties with work or other children will often focus on the shortcomings of the teacher and say he or she is picking on him. This tends to happen more often in large classes with few resources, where the teacher has not made special arrangements for them. These children, especially those who are sensitive, are particularly vulnerable and may find it hard to cope, and may react defensively or aggressively or even withdraw into themselves.

When the child does get upset, give him an outlet for ways of expressing feelings – for example, in physical exercise – or redirect attention to an activity he enjoys to give him a chance to calm down. Encouraging him to count to ten slowly may help him regain self-control before reacting. Getting him to focus on calming his breathing may also help.

Such a vulnerable child may often manage on his own and it is often only in the presence of others in bigger group settings that the problems are noticed. The key to success is for you to encourage support between all children in the class. Rewarding good behaviour, rather than necessarily punishing bad, making a positive comment or smiling can be effective reinforcers.

Children with ADHD benefit from having good programmes for self-esteem enhancement and very clear boundaries for behaviour. Having a less punitive approach and spending time teaching and encouraging will motivate the pupil and reap rewards for both you and child. Strategies suggested in Section 8, such as helping the child feel valued and ideas for nurturing self-esteem, give further information on this.

Recognize that the often intense emotions, coupled with the hypersensitive tendencies of many children with ADHD mean that they may ruminate on issues and situations that have upset them, made them angry or feel humiliated. Sometimes this can last for days or more. They can hold grudges or want to take revenge on those they perceive were responsible and can find it extraordinarily difficult to draw a line and move on to other things.

DEALING WITH VULNERABLE CHILDREN

Impulsive behaviour can result in apparent attention-seeking behaviour. These children seem to always 'be in your face', can't wait their turn, blurt out answers and can appear quite insatiable until they get your attention. It helps to agree with the pupil how often you will work with him – be aware that you may need to do this more frequently than with other pupils to help keep the child with ADHD on task and interested – and to reward only appropriate behaviour with your attention.

Try to minimize the time between the achievement or problem occurring and the praise or punishment that ensues. The longer the time delay the less relevant to the situation it will be for the pupil because of difficulties with understanding cause and effect and short-term memory problems.

Try to bring out the best in the child by rewarding his effort as much as the actual achievement. He will be more likely to cope better if you break down the tasks into manageable chunks and review his progress and new skills learned as much as possible, kindly and encouragingly. Remember that school can be such a struggle for the pupil with ADHD, with little opportunity to escape from what he cannot do well and the expectations on him. Very often this struggle can result in silly behaviour, class clowning, interrupting other pupils and so on, to deflect from a difficult (for him) task or activity and to avoid the fear of failure or humiliation. It is important to read the subtext of this behaviour rather than punish the pupil.

Try focusing on teaching children a set of skills and adaptive behaviours to replace the problem, for example, teach pupils to use materials properly and store them in a desk or locker. Teach aggressive children to develop their sporting talents – replace problem behaviours with positive alternatives.

Because children with ADHD may have trouble reading social cues, body language, voice and tone, unstructured situations and new events may cause problems.

Planning ahead for future activities and assessing the situation with the child with ADHD in mind is necessary because these children find change and unpredicted events particularly unsettling and challenging. This mainly relates to impairments in the ability to think flexibly and creatively, and to be able to adapt to a novel situation.

Children with ADHD need time to adjust and take on board information about a new event or change to their normal routine. Try alerting the child to a change in the normal routine in advance. Think carefully about how far in advance you will need to do this – too early and the child may become fixated on the event and the changes may create anxiety, too late and they won't have time to prepare themselves. You will need to judge this based on your knowledge of the pupil and what has helped or hindered in the past. Speak to the parents, who may have a better idea of how much planning and warning will be necessary. And make sure that all members of staff and parents have adequate information and agree on the amount of detail to give to the child.

Be prepared to be patient – you may need to repeat new information several times before the child is able to assimilate it and his anxiety may mean that he will persist in asking the same questions. It is important to be calm and reassuring about the event. After a while, test the child's knowledge of the event and what he expects by deflecting questions back to him.

In some cases it may be necessary to write down an action plan or timetable for the event, giving details of the demands that will be placed on the child, what he will need to do and when. Events such as school trips or a school play are likely to make him very excited. You may want to establish one or two essential rules about expected behaviour or 'what to do if...' before the event so that he knows what is expected of him and what to do if he starts to feel overwhelmed. It may be necessary to plan for a parent or classroom assistant to be present at the event to offer one-to-one support.

Children with ADHD, even more so than most of us, tend to have very good and very bad days. There is usually no obvious reason for this and it is generally not related to what is going on in their lives, or their diet. It is easy to judge a child with ADHD on his good days or a good piece of work without understanding that his condition means that he cannot be consistent and he is not deliberately 'not trying' on other days. It is useful to realize that this inconsistency is an inherent part of many children's ADHD.

It is also helpful to realize that because pupils with ADHD are simply not ready for the same level of independence and responsibility as their peers, they will need support from their parents and teachers for much longer. They generally need to be treated as being about a third younger than their chronological age. Thus treating a twelve year old in the same way as an eight or nine year old, and having similar expectations of them in your mind, can be a useful strategy. Without this understanding they can be teased, bullied and further rejected by peers. Finding strategies to provide extra support unobtrusively and sensitively, can make all the difference.

GOOD DAYS AND BAD DAYS

One of the main characteristics of children with ADHD is the tendency to act impulsively (acting before thinking about the consequences of their behaviour). Impulsivity often shows itself in a lack of understanding of cause and effect. ADHD pupils can often verbalize the rules but have difficulty internalizing them and translating them into thoughtful behaviour. Difficulties in waiting for what they want also add to the impulsivity. This lack of self-control is probably the primary problem with ADHD. Try to distinguish between premeditated and impulsive behaviours.

Inappropriate comments and/or rude language are common in many of these children and they are sometimes very awkward and tactless socially. They can have a very short fuse. When things go wrong for them they may feel very frustrated and take it out on people and things dearest to them.

Suggestions to help with this include role-playing scenes involving these behaviours, preferably with the child's friends, which can help to identify and practise better ways to solve problems.

Teach pupils with ADHD to slow down before they say things that they'll regret later, and encourage them to practise 'stopping and thinking' before talking. Ask them to wait about five seconds before responding to your questions. This technique can help ADHD pupils a great deal. Identify and set up a support network of peers and adults who can give them hints when they need to slow down and can practise the 'slow down' techniques with them.

Children with ADHD are often so impulsive that when they want to say something, they have to tell you immediately. They also find it difficult to shift quickly from one mindset to another, to organize and make a coherent plan of action to deal with a problem or frustration. They have a poor ability to separate their emotional response to a problem from deciding what they need to do to solve it. They are not good at anticipating problems in advance or the impact of their behaviour on other people.

It helps to appreciate that these children have a reduced capacity for flexibility, adaptability and coping with frustration – more so than other children the same age. Inadequate development of these skills contributes to a variety of behaviours – sudden outbursts, prolonged tantrums, physical and verbal aggression – often in response to the most benign circumstances. This frequently impacts on the child's interactions and relationships with parents, teachers, siblings and peers.

Here are some suggestions for dealing with impulsiveness:

o Keep your behaviour plan simple and flexible. It needs to work for you on a regular basis, and plans that are too complex will not succeed.

o Try to actively monitor your pupil during tests, especially multiple-choice ones. This will help keep him on track, prevent him becoming frustrated or answering at random just to get the test finished.

o Encourage the pupil to check his work, rather than just completing it quickly. Emphasize that this is part of a good work routine. Give instructions on how to do this and encourage him to keep practising.

o In assignments that require research, reports and creative writing, give the pupil a structure and format. For some children dictating the words to someone rather than writing it down initially can be useful, as can be the use of computers. This is especially helpful if the child has difficulties with written language.

When the child remains verbally or physically impulsive and still has persisting concentration difficulties despite appropriate educational strategies, it is advisable to suggest that parents seek advice from their physician about medication.

Warmth, patience and humour – alongside consistency and firmness – will go a long way to counteract the rejection and criticism these children so often experience. Often just a subtle change of approach and tone can reduce stress and promote a more positive relationship between you and the child with ADHD, easing the pressure and making life happier and calmer for everyone.

These children are more likely to listen and take responsibility for their own behaviour when less talk and emotion is used, especially when disciplining the child. You are also likely to punish harder when you are angry and the message to the pupil is that you want to fight.

Consider how the behaviour of others compounds the situation in ADHD. A pupil who is regularly punished for being naughty, singled out for blame and repeatedly told he is a failure will come to believe these things. Sometimes there are years of self-esteem to rebuild. The following ideas are very simple but can make quite a difference.

Instead of saying:

○ 'What on earth did you do such a stupid thing for?' try, 'Tell me why you did that.'
○ 'Be quiet, we are talking!' try, 'Please don't interrupt.'
○ 'I've told you so many times not to do that!' try, 'Please listen carefully.'
○ 'Trust you to always get into trouble,' try, 'Do you want some help?'
○ 'I can't believe you really did that!' try, 'That is quite unacceptable.'
○ 'I'm warning you,' try, 'Please listen to what I am telling you.'
○ 'Stop it!' try, 'I need you to stop what you are doing now.'

PERSISTENT SLOW RATE OF LEARNING

If the child's learning rate remains slow despite appropriate teaching, the situation should be reassessed. It is important to give this feedback to the parents and/or the child's physician so that a medical reassessment can take place at regular monitoring reviews. The child's hearing and vision might need to be checked by a specialist or possibly an evaluation by an educational psychologist might be needed. This requires the teacher to refer the pupil to the special needs teacher and/or child's physician. Consider whether the child is receiving the appropriate level of special needs support and whether he has an individual education plan (IEP) in place.

About a third of children with ADHD have coexisting specific learning difficulties over and above their problems with concentration. There needs to be careful assessment of these and the child's overall level of intelligence in order to understand these difficulties better. The use of medication should not be viewed as a panacea, but it can make a very significant difference to a child's difficulties, and thus his progress.

Children with ADHD and specific learning difficulties need support for both problems. They need support with their ADHD, with structure and an understanding of ADHD, as well as medication where it is considered appropriate by the child's specialist and parents. Support is also required for their specific learning difficulties – their associated dyslexia, mathematics difficulties, handwriting problems, and so on. They are doubly disadvantaged and it is absolutely essential that they are able to concentrate fully so that they can cope better with, and overcome, their associated specific learning difficulties.

It is crucial, therefore, for you to determine the most appropriate, individual support for these children. Target the pupil's areas of weakness and play to his strengths, particularly determining whether he is a stronger visual or auditory learner. A child with short-term memory issues will need repetition and one-to-one support.

By evaluating the child's precise difficulties, a more open-minded and appropriate response to him can be made. Following a specialist educational assessment, the areas in which the pupil needs support can be more clearly identified and you can focus more specifically on these areas of weakness.

Sometimes you can be in the frustrating situation where you are putting in a great deal of support for a pupil, have tried all the most appropriate strategies, and yet the child is still having problems. In such situations it is often a good idea to discuss the matter with an informed colleague and to provide the parents and the physician involved with some feedback, particularly as to whether the core ADHD symptoms are still problematic.

Of course, having ADHD does not exclude other difficulties that could be occurring at school, such as being bullied, having particular friendship problems, or there being marital or other family problems that might be impacting on the child. However, if a pupil with ADHD continues to have problems, is at risk of exclusion or is particularly disruptive or continues to underachieve, then you should work through a mental checklist.

o Are there any other school strategies that could be trialled – sit the pupil at the front of the class or next to better role models, develop a cueing technique, modify teaching delivery style?
o Have there been any bereavements in the family, other stresses, illnesses, sibling problems, etc?
o Does the child look unwell or might he have any other medical condition? If so, suggest a consultation with the child's GP.
o Could there be another complication such as an unrecognized specific learning difficulty or coordination problem?
o Are the core ADHD symptoms appropriately managed?
o Are there other ADHD complications such as severe anxiety, depression, disruptive behaviour or tics that might be hampering educational progress?

Frequently a minor change of attitude or of supportive strategies can be very helpful.

Behavioural difficulties

Although different strategies are helpful in different situations with children and adolescents with ADHD, some of the basic principles for managing behaviour can be particularly relevant to this group of pupils.

o Agree on basic house rules that everyone signs up to. There is then the option of the child choosing to obey the rules – 'Johnny, you know the rules, you have the option of obeying the rule or taking appropriate punishment.'

o Ignore mild inappropriate behaviours and praise those that are more appropriate. Choosing your battles is essential.

o Use effective methods of communicating commands and setting rules. Do not give too many commands at once and frame them positively and specifically. Make the command brief and appropriate to the child's developmental level and give positive attention to the child during this period. Make good eye contact and say his name. State the consequences and follow them through. Use specific situations such as classroom transitions to reinforce these issues.

o Use point/token systems with both reward and cost components to reinforce appropriate behaviour.

o Use a contract with an incentive for achieving set goals (see Idea 43).

o Foreshadow specific problem situations and try to anticipate what is likely to happen.

o Analyse the positive and negative consequences and appropriate and problem behaviours so that there is discussion as to how things might happen better next time.

o When using rewards, use activities that are preferred by the pupil, such as time on the computer or other positive activities, rather than just material rewards.

o When negotiating or drawing up a contract with adolescents, involve the young person in this process as far as possible. Teach them to evaluate their own behaviour and reinforce it themselves.

A contract can be a useful strategy to implement with your ADHD pupil. This is essentially an agreement that is written up between a teacher and pupil regarding problem behaviours. It should explain how the pupil will act or behave differently and what he will receive in return. For example, there might be a contract that states that in return for completing all his homework he will receive a mutually agreed reward. However, there should be short-term goals as well, so that for each of the days when homework is completed he receives a lesser reward.

A contract needn't be a complicated document and could look something like this:

Date: _____

I, _____ agree to do the things listed below.

I will check each day to make sure that I achieve my goal.

	M	T	W	T	F
1					
2					
3					
4					
5					

I, _____ (teacher, parent, or other) agree to provide assistance by

_____

We, _____ and _____, will meet to discuss progress:

_____

(when, how often, and where).

We have read and talked about this contract and are signing it to show that we agree to these terms.

Signatures:

_____ (student)

_____ (teacher)

Options:

The following reward/privilege will be given to the pupil for successfully completing the contract:

_____

_____

(For example, when the student earns five check marks, even if it takes more than a week, he gets reward/privilege provided by either the parents or teacher.)

The pupil will take this contract home to parents at the end of the week.

Because children with ADHD are hypersensitive ar
tend to misinterpret comments, reprimands and
punishments should be done with care and sens.

After an incident, try to put in place appropriate
strategies to prevent similar difficulties recurring. These
should be implemented from an understanding of
ADHD with the aim of minimizing rather than excusing
the behaviour or problem. For example, in a situation
where homework is regularly forgotten or not returned,
arranging for it to be emailed to the teacher might be
an option.

It is usually best to use careful reprimands with a
measured tone of voice and an attitude suited to the
behaviour. Make sure it is clear that it is the behaviour
not the child that you are criticizing and phrase your
comments in such a way as to encourage better
compliance next time. Try not to damage the child's
self-esteem, and avoid appearing stressed, losing control,
lecturing, ridiculing or criticizing the child in front of the
class. Look forward to a positive future by suggesting
ideas as to how things might happen better next time,
and don't see the child as a failure.

MINIMIZE BAD BEHAVIOU'

These pupils can be particularly frustrating to teach and their domineering style often isn't popular with peers. They don't readily back down so it can help to train them to carry out small and reasonable requests and, where possible, give them a choice of outcome, either of which would be acceptable to you. Thus neither party loses face, there is less likelihood of confrontation and the controlling child has not taken over. Give him additional responsibilities that play to his strengths. Many teachers find that asking for the child's help in improving matters can be very productive and encourages further co-operation.

There is every chance that a child behaving badly is suffering inside and his physical, emotional and intellectual performance is being impaired. Do not get drawn into adopting his negative behavioural style, shouting or not bothering with him – this can be persistently draining and can lead you to think that it is you who has the problem. Rather than regarding these pupils as an unwelcome burden, make it a priority to cater for them so that the whole class operates smoothly.

Be conscious of the child, particularly the older pupil, who is unwilling to communicate or looks away when you speak, who paces around, won't remain in his seat and has outbursts of temper. Be aware of tense, rigid body language. Stress levels rapidly rise in many pupils with ADHD and easily get out of control as they tend to have a very short fuse. It is best not to further inflame the situation by confronting the pupil. Try and read the mood of the child before choosing your strategy.

Public outbursts are counterproductive to both you and pupil so try to give him a choice and provide an alternative option to avoid loss of face. Developing non-verbal management strategies, such as finger to lips, pointing to watch, finger to ear, and so on, can help to defuse situations. Focus on the incident – not the pupil.

Don't be afraid to use the 'broken record' technique – keep repeating your message in a calm, non-confrontational tone and try to ensure that your own body language remains calm but assertive. Tell, don't ask. Listen to what the pupil has to say and try to divert his attention using distracting strategies. Humour – used very carefully – can sometimes diffuse a difficult situation. Remember that silence can also be very effective. Refer to rights and responsibilities and express regret for the need to punish. Varying your responses rather than being predictable can also help.

Using 'I', rather than an accusatory 'you' has more chance of success in interacting with pupils with ADHD, who can have a tendency to be especially sensitive to comment and criticism and easily misinterpret or overreact. Potentially inflammatory approaches such as, 'You cleared up the room BUT you didn't close the cupboard doors' could be replaced with more friendly and positive alternatives such as, 'I am pleased you have cleared up the room AND put everything in the cupboard.' Remember, it is often only a change of approach, rather than a need for more resources, that makes the difference in teaching and working with pupils with ADHD.

Bullying causes intense difficulty and misery for many children, both boys and girls, and can occur in a wide variety of ways. All schools have to have a policy on bullying, so make sure that you are familiar with your school's policy.

It's important to find out if there was a specific trigger for the bullying, such as the loss of a best friend or a one-off specific incident. Bullying tends to be a recurrent problem with children with ADHD and if this is the case, going back to basics and reassessing the overall approach to the child's ADHD can be useful. Consider whether social skills support might be necessary, if there is a particular clash with a teacher, if the child's learning difficulties are worse than had been anticipated, or if there might be specific issues at home.

Children with ADHD will often bully others not only because of their innate aggression but also because of their impulsiveness and the fact that they want to be seen as part of a gang due to their social skills difficulties. They may be easily led and sometimes are set up to do the bullying by other children who will later run for cover. Many children with ADHD are adept at spotting weaknesses in another child, and know exactly how to exacerbate a situation, but they may be unaware of the consequences of their actions or may have completely misread the situation They are sometimes surprised at what all the fuss is about.

Alternatively, a child on the receiving end of persistent bullying may well have low self-esteem, social skills difficulties or other issues relating to the more inattentive forms of ADHD.

So, it is well worthwhile thinking about ADHD in both the bully and the bullied. Discussion with the SENCO or behaviour support team would be useful, as well as initiation of appropriate action through the school's bullying policy.

If the child with ADHD is on the receiving end of persistent bullying, aim to use the school's bullying policy as a way of introducing structure, home–school reporting, an action programme, or whatever other action seems appropriate.

If you suspect that your pupil with ADHD is involved in bullying but this is denied, it is important to liaise with the family and to have regular contact with the pupil involved. Bullying involving internet chat rooms and mobile phones is becoming increasingly common and such forms of bullying can be quite insidious and difficult to detect. Showing support and understanding for the pupil will help to sort things out.

DISRUPTIVE BEHAVIOUR

Persistent disruptive behaviour can be very draining and demoralizing for you and difficult for the rest of the class. It may lead to school suspension or exclusion. If such a child remains disruptive and/or oppositional with frequent arguing, defying and pushing the school boundaries, even when medically treated for ADHD, specialist consideration should be given to whether the child might have associated oppositional defiant disorder. It is not uncommon for these symptoms to be worse in the home setting. They often improve when the core ADHD symptoms are treated.

If these problems are persistent, initially discuss with parents or colleagues whether any medication changes might be considered by the medical staff, and also whether any additional behavioural strategies might be necessary, as well as many of the previously mentioned educational strategies. Generally, self-esteem and social skills difficulties will not improve until this is effectively managed.

Other strategies worth trialling with these pupils include methods of communicating commands and rules by making eye contact with the pupil and saying his name, not giving too many instructions at once and framing the instructions positively and specifically. It is important to make the instructions brief and appropriate to the pupil's developmental level, stating the consequences and following them through.

It can also be worth trying the use of daily charts leading to points and tokens. Try to foreshadow specific problem situations and, especially in the younger child, use the 'time-out' method. With adolescents, negotiating a contract can be helpful.

While there are many reasons for children being suspended or excluded from school, pupils with ADHD and associated disruptive behavioural difficulties are much more likely to be so. Once suspended or excluded, or if possible in the lead up to this, consideration must be given as to whether or not an assessment is necessary to evaluate whether a condition such as ADHD is present.

The simplistic assumption that disruptive behaviour leading to exclusion is always the result of family or socio-economic difficulties must be dispelled. While this may be true in some cases, it can also be due to the presence of recognized conditions such as ADHD.

It is therefore wise for teachers to collate information to consider whether the child has, over the years, been persistently inattentive, hyperactive or impulsive, either verbally or physically, and whether this could have contributed to the suspension or expulsion.

Give careful consideration, following an assessment, even if it is done at a late stage in the child's school career, as to whether or not the pupil can be effectively managed within mainstream schooling. Effective management can often make all the difference and enable a child to behave better and achieve more. Indeed, such an assessment can be part of the rehabilitation process and should involve the special educational needs department, and educational psychologist as well as a medical specialist.

SCHOOL SUSPENSION/EXCLUSION

Helping the pupil with organization

Many children with ADHD have persistent problems with planning, organization and time management, irrespective of whether they are on medication or not. Problems with prioritizing, making decisions, thinking ahead and having a concept of time are common and can cause a great deal of difficulty in the school setting. Children with these difficulties need as much structure, support and 'scaffolding' as possible. In particular, there needs to be a recognition that these problems are part of the child's ADHD.

Remember that a pupil with ADHD will need the sort of support typically used for a younger child (as much as a third younger than their chronological age), so, for example, a twelve year old needs the level of support and understanding normally given to an eight year old, such as the parent and teacher taking responsibility for checking and organizing their backpack.

Pupils with ADHD tend to live entirely in the present. They are not able to efficiently bring the experience from the past to decision-making today, nor are they able to think of possible outcomes in the future based on current performance. In short, planning, setting priorities and carrying through a long-term project to completion are challenging for ADHD pupils and become increasingly disabling as they rise through the school system. Such difficulties do not typically respond to medication, although they do continue to improve into early adulthood. However, in the meantime, skills need to be taught and the pupils supported with strategies to compensate for their weaknesses if their work is not to be affected.

Persistent organizational difficulties can often appear to be within the child's control and such children are often regarded as lazy or unmotivated. It is important to understand that these weaknesses are part of the ADHD picture and are not the 'fault' of the child, the teacher or the parent.

Try to be aware of and minimize the impact of a child's disorganization on his schooling and life difficulties. If a child is receiving recurrent detentions or punishments for not completing homework or having other organizational difficulties such as being late for lessons, identify the main reasons this is happening and put in place strategies to help minimize this. Specific strategies will depend on exactly what the problem is. They may involve support with a home–school diary, making sure the child writes his homework down in class, emailing the homework back to the teacher, liaising with the parents, or possible medication changes. It is therefore important to institute appropriate strategies to try to prevent the difficulty recurring, rather than punishing the pupil and risking a negative effect on his self-esteem.

GETTING SORTED FOR HOMEWORK

Homework can be particularly difficult for children with ADHD, largely because of their problems with prioritizing, planning, organization and time management. Difficulties getting things down in writing and problems with memory can also contribute. Medication can wear off towards the end of the school day or just after school, and if the child is not taking medication to cover homework time, this can compound the difficulties.

You need to be clear regarding the purpose of the homework and the date due. Give out the homework assignment at the beginning of class and make sure that it is recorded in the assignment book or planner by all pupils when you have their attention. Too often, teachers give out assignments during the last two minutes of class when the ADHD pupil has lost focus and is preparing to move to the next class. Guidance should be given as to the format and what other additional materials or other resources might be necessary. Check that the pupils have understood the assignment, and have written it down, and, if possible, provide time in the classroom when the assignment or homework can be started under some supervision. As much as possible homework should reinforce or extend what is being done at school that day.

Writing assignments on Post-it notes and placing these in the pupil's assignment book can also work well, with each teacher/subject having a different colour Post-it. Try to check daily that assignments are recorded in the assignment book and, if possible, get another pupil to help with this.

Getting all the right books home is often a headache for pupils. Many solve this problem by taking all their books with them everywhere, resulting in extremely heavy backpacks. Sometimes – financial considerations notwithstanding – it can be useful to have a duplicate set of textbooks at home. Having the pupil record necessary books in an assignment book may work for a few. In primary school, if parents are collecting their child from school, they may be able to check assignments and which books are needed before heading home.

Because homework can be such a nightmare for pupils with ADHD, parents may appreciate some general advice on how best to support their child. Suggest that they try some of the following ideas:

○ Set a daily routine with clearly understood (and written down) times for starting homework, break-times and finishing time.

○ Use a timer or an alarm clock to announce these times (so that it is not the mother doing it!). Keep the time short and achievable, gradually lengthening it as the child is able. If the child is working on the computer, alarms can be set on the computer to announce stretch breaks.

○ Have a snack and an exercise break before starting homework.

○ Always do 'work' in the same 'work place' and do not allow play activity in that location. If the child needs a break they should leave the 'work place'. Some children may need several 'work places' for different types of work, such as reading and writing.

○ Allow the child to write while lying on the floor – some children with ADHD prefer writing with their whole body supported by the floor.

○ Provide a tray with all the necessary supplies (pens, calculator, scissors, stapler, paper, and so on) that can be moved to whichever 'work place' is being used. This saves time looking for stuff and getting distracted.

○ Help them to get started – many children need direct supervision to get the first sentence/problem completed and can then work with less supervision.

○ Be available for help. Most children do better doing homework in a place where there is obvious supervision in range – maybe an open door with a parent passing by regularly or doing homework on the dining room table where the parent is in view.

GETTING HOMEWORK DONE

- o Record the time taken to achieve an assignment – this will help the child to learn to pace himself and to provide a level of understanding between parent and teacher on homework completion. With good communication between parent and teacher, homework assignments may be based on time rather than quantity.
- o Make sure that the internet is disconnected when homework is to be done. If the internet is required for the assignment, make sure that 'instant messaging' and any games are not available.
- o Consider allowing the child to wear headphones to block out auditory distractions – some will do better with music playing, others will do better with headphones and no music.
- o Homework done on a computer should be backed up on a disk, flash-drive or the internet and printed out so that if it gets lost it can be duplicated.
- o Having the child sit next to a non-ADHD sibling or friend while doing his homework will help to build expectations.
- o When each assignment is complete, ensure that it is placed immediately in the child's bag or backpack in an agreed location.

If the parent or child becomes too stressed over the homework then a well-supervised homework club at school could be the answer. It may be easier for a pupil to do homework at school because they see school as being somewhere where they are used to having more structure than at home.

Remembering homework and getting it back to school can be very difficult for ADHD pupils. A regular daily routine is needed for handing in homework at the beginning of the class. The teacher should request the homework assignment at the start of the class and supervise the pupil until it is found and handed in. Liaison with parents is very important so that the exact cause of the problem can be ascertained and appropriate accommodations put in place.

Many children with ADHD do particularly good work on the computer but can forget to hand it in. Having the ability to email homework direct to the teacher can be a way of short-circuiting these difficulties. There are issues with additional work for the teacher. However, experience shows that if the system is well organized this generally does not create too much extra work and can in fact minimize much of the frustration felt by both teacher and child.

Of course, having children working on computers with online capability has its own problems. Passwords need to be used and due regard given to safe internet use.

There need to be rules regarding whether or not the child may ask the teacher questions or expect too much of the teacher. However, the basic idea of emailing homework to the teacher is something well worth considering. You could also think about posting assignments on the internet or emailing assignments to the pupil's home and the pupil can email them back after completion.

HANDING HOMEWORK IN

IMPROVING WORKING MEMORY

Short-term memory problems, over and above concentration difficulties, often improve with the use of medication. However, if such difficulties persist despite the child being on medication, it may sometimes indicate that liaison by the parent or teacher with the child's physician for further advice about fine-tuning the medication is necessary.

Appropriate educational strategies should also be geared to whether a child responds better using vision or hearing. Some children with ADHD have associated persistent auditory processing difficulties and they will be best presented with visual materials. Most ADHD pupils are visual and kinaesthetic learners – they learn best by seeing and doing.

Many of the ideas for improving short-term and working memory are similar to those outlined previously for improving attention and concentration. They include:

o Pre-teach the general outline of new information and guide the pupil's attention to listen for important points before teaching the rest of the lesson.

o Repeat instructions or new information so that the pupil can increase the amount of information captured.

o Establish eye contact with the pupil prior to giving essential instructions or new material – this will help to ensure that he is ready to listen carefully.

o Consider altering the rate of presentation of new material as the pupil may need additional processing time or more time to rehearse the information.

o Where possible, break the tasks or information down into small steps or chunks.

The pupil with ADHD's focus is likely to fade more quickly than his peers'. Changing tasks more frequently can alleviate some of the drain on sustained working memory.

A child with difficulties sustaining working memory often needs frequent short breaks. Breaks typically need only be one or two minutes in duration. Observing when the pupil's ability to focus begins to wane will help determine the optimal time for a break. Breaks are best taken with a motor activity or a relaxing activity – the child might walk to the pencil sharpener, run a short errand, get a drink or simply bring his work to show you.

Get the pupil to check in with you on a regular basis. This can be an effective method of providing a break with motor activity and an opportunity for reinforcement. The child might be asked to complete only a few problems of a set or a few lines of a paragraph before bringing his work to you for review.

Try to avoid lengthy tasks, particularly those that the pupil sees as tedious or monotonous. Intersperse them with more frequent breaks or other, more engaging tasks. The pupil might be rewarded with a more stimulating activity, such as computer instruction time, for completing the more tedious task.

Recognize that competing information can have quite a negative impact on working memory. It is therefore important to reduce distractions in the environment that can tax or disrupt sustained working memory. Think about your seating plan and avoid seating the child near a noisy corridor or window and keep him away from the more distracting children in the classroom. You could consider the use of headphones to minimize distractions.

Try to seat the child with ADHD near you so that there is increased supervision and a greater opportunity to observe when he is adequately focused and when he is tiring, and redirection or breaks can be more easily implemented.

Often pupils with problems with working memory also exhibit word and information retrieval difficulties. They frequently experience the 'tip of the tongue' phenomenon, or may produce the wrong details within the correct concept. These pupils may need additional time to retrieve details when answering a question. They often benefit from presentation of information in several different modes.

Give verbal instructions accompanied by visual cues, demonstration and guidance to increase the likelihood that new material will be learned.

Use mnemonic devices (memory strategies) to help the pupil learn, and later recall, basic skills and facts.

Rehearsal is often a helpful method of increasing the amount of information encoded into memory. Have the pupil repeat or paraphrase what he has heard or understood in order to check for accuracy and to provide an opportunity for rehearsal. Remember, little and often is best.

Try to help the pupil learn how to actively listen. Get him routinely to stop what he is doing, then focus his attention, ask him questions and get him to restate the information or question and take notes.

Having a coach or mentor is a very important strategy in managing a child with ADHD. This person could be another teacher, an older pupil, or possibly someone from outside the school environment.

A coach or mentor needs to be a person who believes in the child with ADHD, has some understanding of the condition and is able to meet him either in person or by phone on a regular basis, to encourage and to help with planning and progress generally.

Because children with ADHD tend very much to think in the 'here and now' and not plan ahead, one of the key roles of the coach is to structure, think ahead, organize and foreshadow forthcoming events, and to help the child think his way through them – remember his PE kit or the directions for football games, and so on. The coach can also be very helpful in reminding, encouraging and helping the child stay focused and on task.

When the child has a bad day, the coach has a role to play in providing encouragement, helping to avoid procrastination, and getting organized and minimizing negative, destructive thinking. All this helps to boost the child's self-esteem and promote social skills.

Pupil and coach should have a regular, at least weekly, meeting in the same time slot, for between 15–30 minutes. There needs to be an agenda and this is often best done using a notebook where items discussed are written down, and these can then be reviewed at the next meeting. The previous week needs to be looked at and analysed as to where problems occurred, what might have been done to help, and general encouragement given. The next week is then planned, potential pitfalls identified, and as much praise and support provided as possible.

Working with a coach or mentor can provide a 'stepping stone' effect; it can be very useful as a non-medical strategy for ADHD and is very effective in promoting self-esteem, organizational and social skills.

Specific learning difficulties

HELP WITH ACADEMIC SKILLS

When a child has ongoing academic difficulties over and above those caused by the core ADHD symptoms of poor concentration, impulsivity and hyperactivity, he may need specific support in these areas. While detailed discussion of specific learning difficulties is beyond the scope of this book, there are some broad principles to be aware of that may help the child achieve to his ability.

First, the child will need to be placed on the school's Special Needs Support Register, usually at the School Action stage, the first stage of the Special Educational Needs Code of Practice, so that additional targeted support is available at school. A range of strategies is available in the Code of Practice, so that specific learning difficulties (dyslexia, and numeracy, sometimes referred to as dyscalculia) are properly targeted. Some strategies might include:

o Additional reading time if reading is weak – use 'previewing' strategies; the selection of text with fewer words on a page and shortening the amount of required reading.

o When oral expression is weak – encourage the child to talk about new ideas or experiences, pick topics that are easy for the child to talk about, try and give him the confidence to speak out in class.

o When written language is weak – try to provide structure and help with sequencing and an overall framework for the writing. Using word processors, laptops, displays and projects can be helpful. Don't give him large quantities of written work to do and try to use multiple-choice or fill-in questions in tests.

o When mathematics is weak – allow the use of calculators with display screens, use graph paper to space numbers, provide additional time, immediate feedback and instruction via modelling of the correct computational methods.

It is a good idea for teachers to clarify what is meant by 'dyslexia' in an individual child. Unfortunately, the term dyslexia is sometimes inappropriately used to cover a wide range of learning difficulties. This is often not particularly helpful for the child. True dyslexia is a language-based learning disability specifically related to reading. There are many other types of specific learning difficulties.

If a child in your class has a label of dyslexia, consider whether the term has been appropriately used, as this may influence the teaching strategies you implement. He may also have features of, for example, ADHD and/or Tourette Syndrome and/or handwriting difficulties, and this may have led to an inappropriate diagnosis.

Helpful strategies for the child with dyslexia include teaching phonological awareness, including sound discrimination and identification, syllables and rhyme, and hearing sounds within words. The letter–sound links should also be taught in a structured, cumulative and multi-sensory way. These children need frequent reminders and revision of what has been learned.

If the child has difficulty expressing ideas, then try using visualization techniques, keep a vocabulary book and use story tapes.

Make sure that the reading tasks are appropriate for the skill and comprehension levels of the pupil, while at the same time being interesting and challenging. Also, highlight key words and instructions on worksheets, using large well-spaced type, with visuals and short sentences.

Use a range of approaches to accommodate different styles of thinking and learning. For visual learners, make use of plenty of visual material, overhead projectors, video and interactive whiteboards. For auditory learners, use a range of social interactions, discussions, questions and answers, word pictures and auditory memory games. For kinaesthetic learning styles, the pupil will require lots of different ways of gathering information, looking, listening, hands-on exploration and experimentation. For children with auditory working memory difficulties it can be helpful to use a range of memory strategies and games, mnemonics and, if necessary, to use a dictaphone.

For pupils who struggle with written work, look for alternative methods of recording such as developing touch-typing skills, using a computer, tape recorder, dictaphone, scribe or possibly voice-recognition software.

When a child has seen an educational psychologist (EP) the key points from that assessment should be used to draw up a classroom strategy plan. The report should provide a base point for the development of appropriate teaching strategies.

When you are interpreting the EP's report, start with the summary or overview at the end of the report to gain a broad picture of the child's difficulty. Determine which definition of dyslexia is being used and whether or not the psychologist appears to have considered the possibility of ADHD, autistic spectrum difficulties, and so on, or whether the report makes assumptions or hypotheses which might come from a predetermined professional standpoint.

Then look at both the overall IQ scores and the percentiles they are on. Note whether there is a significant discrepancy between the verbal and performance IQ scores, and where the child's IQ is on the percentiles – i.e. if a child is very bright, or in the lower IQ range. This is useful in determining whether your perception of the child's intellectual ability might have been an over- or underestimate. However, some children with ADHD tend to underscore on IQ testing, probably because of the timed element and the problems with concentration, despite the fact that these are allowed for to some extent.

Other children may underachieve during assessment because of oppositionality or anxiety on the day of the assessment. Look at whether the working memory and processing speed scores are commensurate with the other scores or, as is often the case if ADHD is present, they are much lower. Also look at the attainments and whether they are both at an appropriate age level, and also relative to the child's IQ. Frequently, a child with ADHD will have attainments that are two to three years behind expectations; however, when a child has specific learning difficulties in association with ADHD, the gap is often wider.

Note carefully the conclusions, and analyse the reasons for these conclusions being made. Is there any discrepancy in the report between what you notice in the classroom and what has been noted in the one-to-one setting of the assessment? If there are significant discrepancies, it is worth having a conversation with the EP about this.

Finally, read through the recommendations and develop an action plan to deliver these in the classroom. Be certain that the child with ADHD and specific learning difficulties is on the correct stage of the Code of Practice and that the appropriate support strategies are recorded and evaluated using an individual education plan.

Mathematics can be very challenging for children with
ADHD. Their weaknesses with short-term memory mean
that they often have difficulty in retrieving the basic
principles of addition, subtraction, multiplication and
division. They may not have learned the basic building
blocks of mathematics, especially if their ADHD was
diagnosed late. They struggle to hold numbers and
information in their minds while they perform the
calculation.

It is important to allow the other pupils in the class to
move on at an appropriate rate, but to give the child with
ADHD ways to gradually develop the basic building
blocks. Try to help the pupil focus on mastering the basic
principles and concepts rather than having to struggle
with the difficulty of memorizing the skills and the
numbers.

You will find that your ADHD pupil's work is often
messy and he may have problems lining up numbers and
putting columns in the correct place, as well as carrying
numbers from one column to the next. This may be
exacerbated by poor handwriting. The child may need
support to write the numbers down, rather than doing
the calculations in his head. This means he may miss
steps and make careless errors while he rushes through
the work.

It can be a good idea to modify mathematics
assignments so that rather than doing all the problems,
the pupil is asked to do every other problem. Try to
reduce the amount of writing that is necessary and
photocopy the pages for the child, possibly enlarging
them to allow more room for his working out. The pupil
may need to keep a model of the problem that is being
solved written on a separate piece of paper or a coloured
card so that he can refer back to it when he forgets.

In some situations a calculator with a display screen may
be used once the pupil has grasped the basic concepts.
He must, however, understand the basic mathematics skills,
especially for trigonometry and algebra.

Other ways to help the pupil with ADHD struggling with mathematics include using mnemonics, allowing extra time for assignments and supporting organizational and sequencing skills.

Handwriting problems

About 50% of pupils with ADHD also have developmental coordination disorder (DCD). This combination is commonly seen in the classroom as illegible or slow handwriting (dysgraphia).

Computers are often the long-term answer to illegible handwriting, but learning good keyboard skills can be just as frustrating for a child as it requires the same coordination skills that prevent them from writing well. For ADHD pupils computers are usually easier to focus on than handwriting books, and most pupils can learn to type with time and encouragement. Ideally, young children should start typing using a ten-finger method from the beginning to prevent learning with two fingers and then having to unlearn it later. Keyboard skills should be taught alongside handwriting from the earliest opportunity.

Younger children can learn to type as they learn to read, using programs such as *Read, Write and Type* (www.readwriteandtype.com). Older pupils can learn keyboard skills using any of the good computer-based typing programs readily available. They need to practise regularly, little and often (for example, 15 minutes, five times a week), rather than one long session per week. Most pupils will benefit from a reward system built in by the parents to give immediate rewards for successful participation in the program.

Most ADHD pupils need to learn these skills before they are typically taught in school and they will need more tuition time and support than non-ADHD pupils. Instant messaging (as long as it is closely supervised) is a wonderful incentive for pupils to learn to type.

A minimum speed of 20 words per minute is necessary in order for a computer to be less frustrating to a pupil than using a pencil. You may find that computer typing programs are too difficult for some children as they go too fast, so the solution is to resort to the old-fashioned typing manuals, which go at their speed.

Generally, a laptop computer for a pupil with ADHD in the classroom is an expensive risk and an added distraction. Cheaper solutions are available, such as the portable word processor, the AlphaSmart (www.AlphaSmart.com) or similar. For some pupils the typing programs that come with these word processors are easier for them to learn as they can go at their own pace.

It may be necessary to cover the keyboard to break the habit of looking at their hands when they type, which is common with children with poor motor planning skills. This slows the motor learning process down, as it does not matter which finger hits which key on the keyboard. There are a number of ways to achieve this – one of the best is using a specially made skin that fits over the computer keys. This can be bought through www.speedskin.com/ Alternatively, use a box to cover the keyboard of a desktop computer with cut-outs for the hands, or place the keyboard inside a pair of men's boxer shorts at the waist end and then place the hands through the legs of the shorts.

Illegible handwriting or dysgraphia is very common in pupils with ADHD. The ability to write requires many complex developmental systems to be in place and it is important to consider whether there may be a developmental coordination disorder (DCD) alongside the ADHD. It may be helpful for the child to see an occupational therapist. Sometimes, however, the difficulty in writing things down is due to oppositional behaviour or boredom ('Why should I write it down if I can say it straight away?') and sometimes due to short-term memory issues or problems with written expression. Working on the computer is often helpful in this situation. However, there are a few things you can do to make handwriting easier.

POSTURE

o Make sure that the child has a chair and table/desk that are the appropriate size for him and that he faces the teacher and the whiteboard. His feet should be on the floor; ankles, knees, hips and elbows should be as close to right angles as possible.

o A slightly sloped writing surface encourages extension at the wrists and improves dexterity. This can be accomplished by attaching the child's exercise book to a closed two- or three-inch ring binder with the raised edge away from the child. A piece of non-slip rubber mat (such as Dycem) on the bottom prevents the file from moving about on the desk, and another under the exercise book or paper will stop that from moving – a bulldog clip attached to the binder can serve the same purpose.

PAPER

o This needs to be positioned correctly so that the child can see what he is writing. When the child sits with both elbows on the desk with hands together so that they form a right angle, a right-handed child should align the top of the paper with the left arm in this position and the left-handed child should align it with the right arm. A piece of masking tape on the desk to remind child and teacher of the paper position can be useful. This is extremely important for left-handed pupils who frequently develop a 'hooked hand' when writing on poorly positioned paper.

○ The paper needs to be of good enough quality that writing is a pleasing experience, whatever implement is used.

○ Use the line width to match the pupil's handwriting size – this may mean using the exercise books used for younger pupils.

THE RIGHT TOOLS

Before your pupil starts writing, ensure that he is using the right sort of pen or pencil.

PENCIL/PEN

o Use a good quality tool that works for the child. Have plenty of spares, as the ADHD child loses pens and pencils!

o The best quality coloured pencils, markers or crayons should be used to minimize frustration for the child.

o A pencil with a larger shaft is easier to manipulate. The shaft can be increased by using a pencil grip or by taping three pencils together with the writing one slightly longer than the other two.

o Triangular pencils do not roll off desks as easily.

o A felt-tip handwriting pen may be easier for a child with a heavy grip who frequently breaks pencil leads.

o A good quality felt-tip handwriting pen is less messy than a fountain pen and gives much the same appearance.

PENCIL GRIP

Children with ADHD often have immature neuromuscular control and are made to write before their hands are sufficiently developed. As a result they often develop strange pencil grips. Once habituated (usually by the age of seven years) it is very hard to change these grips, even when they have mature neuromuscular control. However, many go on to write successfully with strange grips, which though not ideal as they can cause hand problems later in life, are usually adequate in these days of computers.

The younger child will need repeated prompting to hold the pencil with the 'proper grip'. The important aspect of the grip is that there is a space between the thumb and first finger so that they can move the pencil in opposition to each other, with the second finger providing support under the pencil. If the space between the thumb and first finger is closed, as in a child fisting the hand around the pencil, then increasing the size of the pencil shaft should help.

If the child with ADHD is experiencing handwriting problems or is finding handwriting boring, there are a number of creative solutions you could employ:

○ Allow more space – when making worksheets, allow for bigger handwriting, as the child's immature handwriting is often larger than that of the peer group. Use the enlarger on the photocopier to make larger copies for the ADHD/dysgraphic pupil.

○ Use exercise books for younger pupils where the lines are spaced further apart or have the pupil write on every other line to improve legibility.

○ If squared paper is not available for mathematics then use lined paper in landscape so that the writing lines form columns to help line up numbers.

○ Keep cups full of different pencils/pens and when the ADHD child is becoming bored, place the cup on his desk and ask him to use a different pen for each word or sentence. This gives him something to fiddle with, slows him down and keeps him focused on the writing task.

○ Use coloured paper or coloured pens/markers/crayons instead of just pencil – the use of colour helps hold the pupil's attention. Using black paper and gel pens is a way to bring variety to routine (boring) writing practice.

○ Cut out interesting paper shapes in coloured paper for spelling lists.

○ Use individual blackboard slates and chalk to teach handwriting. Use small pieces of chalk and small pieces of sponge to clean the chalk marks. This develops the fine motor control skills needed for penmanship. White boards are too slippery and do not provide the sensory feedback of chalk, necessary for motor learning.

Other creative ideas include involving other pupils as note-takers and allowing the pupil to dictate answers. In rare cases speech-enabled computer software can be useful. These strategies can be implemented where the child significantly underachieves with the written word compared to verbal expression.

MAKE HANDWRITING MORE FUN!

Poor handwriting can impact on a child's self-esteem and, typically, children who have problems with handwriting are very aware of their lack of skill and will try to avoid it. The risk is that they have a paragraph of knowledge in their heads but are only prepared to put a sentence on paper. Like all aspects of learning, a sense of success builds self-confidence and encourages new learning. The challenge for you is to find a way for poor writers to feel successful, while encouraging them to improve. This can be done by:

o not drawing attention to poor writing
o giving clear expectations as to when 'best writing' is required and allowing less good writing at other times
o reducing the quantity of 'best writing' required and giving praise for those samples
o allowing more time for 'best writing'. When speed is required, allow for less legible output
o encouraging keyboard skills.

Allow the pupil to dictate to another adult (teaching assistant or parent) when the 'content' is what is being evaluated.

Enhancing self-esteem and social skills

CHILDREN NEED TO FEEL VALUED

Most children with ADHD gradually, even with excellent home and school support, have some decrease in self-esteem and confidence. They may also become demotivated. The struggle and difficulty they have with their work usually means that within two to three years of starting school – sometimes sooner – self-esteem can become more fragile. It is essential to provide support and protection for self-esteem.

Careful listening, sharing and caring can help a child feel valued, as can giving the child your undivided attention. Saying 'yes' rather than 'I'll do it later' can be very important.

Encourage children with ADHD to have a sense of belonging, loyalty and responsibility to a larger group, and to contribute and feel connected to it. It is a good idea to ask their help for specific tasks, whether this is in the family, at school, in a sports club, at cubs or in an orchestra. Children with low self-esteem tend to feel isolated and worthless. Those around them need to help them feel they are contributing to a larger group and are valued within it.

Schools need to encourage all pupils to feel 'connected' by allowing time in the curriculum to meet in tutor groups, assemblies, matches, art exhibitions, musical events, cooking for the staff, woodwork demonstrations, and so on – and not just the very talented. Allow all children to participate, especially those who would not usually get an opportunity. If they are less able and won't be selected to play in the A team or the orchestra, another team or group should be formed where such children can participate and feel involved. All pupils should be involved with an activity in which they would be letting the rest of the group down if they did not turn up, had not learned their lines or remembered their instrument, etc.

Ask for the child's suggestions as to what he thinks would help him to remember to learn his lines/bring his musical instrument and turn up at the right time, on the right day. Enlist the help of his parents in establishing and implementing suitable strategies. Encourage him to appreciate how he might feel if another pupil let him or other members of the group down and also what effect this would have on the activity. Help him to understand how important his role is to everyone's overall enjoyment and let him see that you are genuinely interested in the part he plays in the group. Ask him about it. Show him the importance of being reliable. Remember to praise him for his commitment and efforts to become a valued member of the group.

RECOGNIZING POTENTIAL

Children with ADHD tend to be more impaired than their peers in school behaviour, academic progress and social interaction with peers and parents. The various impairments of these children, their difficulties with school behaviour, organizing their spare time and relationships with parents often mean that their true potential and ability are not recognized. Their lack of motivation may mean that they tend to spend more time unproductively around the house. Relationship difficulties with parents and at school may mean that life can be a very negative experience for them, without support or understanding. All children need nurturing, but those with ADHD require this in abundance to be able to function fully to their potential.

It's important to recognize that these children may need sensitive help in making and maintaining friendships. Try to help them counteract the effects that their whirlwind behaviour or impulsiveness may have on others and understand how this may discourage friendships. There is no easy way to do this, but developing a relationship with the child, pointing out where specific situations have been problematic and making suggestions for the future can often be helpful.

Children with ADHD tend to get blamed more than other children, and sometimes can have a reputation for always being in trouble which goes before them, so they are blamed for things that are not even their fault. They can often be bullied or bully and, sometimes, in a desperate attempt to make friends, try to 'buy' them with toys or sweets. Sadly, that type of 'friendship' can be very short lived as the other child soon loses interest. Very often they don't get invited to parties, included in the football team and can even be excluded from school outings.

So, make a point of highlighting – to them and often in front of others – their areas of competence as well as their areas of knowledge. This can be particularly motivating and encouraging to these vulnerable pupils.

Usually, there is something that the child will do very well. When you discover it, try to emphasize the achievements, without being patronizing. This will give him more confidence, and nothing succeeds like success.

Try to steer the child to accomplish smaller tasks. A job well done, however small, is better than a huge project unfinished. Independence is to be encouraged, but children with ADHD especially need adults to support them and provide security.

Listen carefully to the child with ADHD and be aware that he is very prone to misreading situations and can overreact and readily become upset. This can make him an easy target for other children.

Try to share his view of the situation and adopt an empathetic, supportive approach. Aim to encourage a sense of belonging to the class and to the school, and of making a contribution. Support him in his activities, both within and outside the school and praise and acknowledge even apparently relatively minor achievements. Involving the child in something, even if it is to look after the school guinea pigs or be a milk monitor, is helpful. If he is not good enough to play in the best teams or be in the school play, then some way of acknowledging and encouraging his strengths and abilities should be found.

Try not to let the child feel different, and enable him to work and behave to his ability. It is more likely that with appropriate support his other abilities will also become apparent and flourish.

Frequently, the child with ADHD tends to elicit negative and controlling behaviour from adults, rather than supportive and positive behaviour. This means that his name has often gone before him and he may more readily be blamed for the misdemeanours of others. Be careful to discipline respectfully and sensitively. Do not change the rule but use polite enforcement. Pupils do not like to be 'told off' by teachers whom they hold in high regard. Conversely, they often find it difficult to accept praise from teachers who they perceive as treating them with contempt or disrespect.

Try to ensure the pupil has confidence in the adults who are around him. For example, if he is upset with something that has happened at school or at a club, don't deny the problem but be understanding and supportive. Only then discuss why it happened and offer ways to avoid it happening again. Do not blame others in front of the child. If you need to, speak to the teacher or a parent in private, but try not to show your disappointment in front of the child in how the situation was handled.

Children need to know that someone is on their side who believes in them, which does not mean that the person is a 'soft touch'. On the contrary, they care enough to correct things quickly and act as the child's brakes when theirs have failed. Say 'no' and mean 'no'. Discipline should be consistent and within defined boundaries.

BUILDING CONFIDENCE

NURTURING SELF-ESTEEM

Not many children with ADHD have good self-esteem because their difficulties can often lead to frequent failure, being rejected and/or punished. It is important to put in place nurturing strategies where they can achieve in order to build their self-esteem, which in turn will increase their confidence in themselves.

Because children with ADHD tend to find coping with planning a situation problematic, they may need help to create a structure for attaining their goals. It can help them to feel in control and 'in the driving seat', even if 'steering' is difficult. However, because some children with ADHD are particularly hypersensitive, there is a fine line between being viewed as too patronizing and not praising enough.

Try to understand the child's areas of vulnerability. Give lots of reassurance to build confidence and ability. Praise his efforts to learn. Encourage the concept that learning is not always easy and can at times be a struggle, and for the child to view mistakes and failures as part of learning rather than to feel deflated by them.

Avoid taking away the thing that he does well – football, swimming, riding his bike, and so on. Don't say things like, 'You have been so badly behaved today, I'm afraid you will not be playing for the football team on Friday.' The child with ADHD will not see the connection unless it is immediate and such an approach will tend to alienate you from the child and be counter-productive.

Encourage pupils with ADHD to help other children. Because they are often more comfortable with older or younger children, it can be helpful for them to mix more with other age groups to boost confidence.

Try to establish for yourself whether the child with ADHD actually has a certain coping skill or has understood what is being asked of him/how to do something and, if not, teach it to him as you would any other skill.

For example, revising is often boring for children with ADHD and has no clear short-term goals. Many such pupils just do not understand what is involved and have difficulty in structuring their time. An understanding of this difficulty means that you may be able to put in place a plan and short-term goals to help them.

Children with ADHD frequently lose things. If a child has lost his school bag, rather than saying 'I'll find it for you', suggest that you will help him look for it but emphasize that it is his responsibility and he needs to be involved. Then set up a strategy to keep the bag safe in the future, such as keeping it in a locker in the classroom, and jointly make a decision as to how to improve things for future situations. You will promote a much happier environment for yourself and the child if you teach and support him with a genuine understanding of his struggle with everyday things the rest of us take for granted.

Remember that there is a fine line between providing appropriate accommodations for a child and promoting self-reliance, so these strategies need to be implemented carefully.

IMPROVING SOCIAL SKILLS

Although effective medical management of a child with ADHD often improves social skills difficulties, some children have persistent problems that may be further helped by social skills groups.

Social skills difficulties in these children are not only caused by impulsive comments or actions, but also by their dogmatism or rigid thinking and their poor listening skills or lack of focus. Sometimes their high energy levels can make it difficult for their peers to keep up.

However, there are some pupils with ADHD who have good social skills, who are the life and soul of the party and who have many friends, but often have difficulty with more intimate or close relationships. These difficulties mean that they can frequently be socially isolated and unhappy.

When pupils with ADHD have persistent difficulty picking up on social cues, or act impulsively and are unaware of their effect on others, it can be helpful to enlist the support of peers in the classroom, especially those with good social awareness. Pair them with an ADHD pupil and use them as a 'study buddy' for activities and projects.

Because these ADHD pupils rarely learn from experience socially and will often say embarrassing things to peers and have fairly unstructured conversation, put in place strategies such as counting to three before calling out in class, or involve the child in group work where he can work with others in completing assignments and projects, encouraging them to share organizational ideas and responsibilities.

Children with ADHD are happier and calmer if they know what to expect. They have difficulty monitoring situations and themselves at the same time or adjusting their action to the setting. They are less able to interpret emotions in others or identify emotions in themselves and be able to predict what will happen next. They often have problems with managing frustration and tend to overreact to (often minor to the observer) wants, hurts and worries.

Try to anticipate potentially problematic situations in advance as these children can rapidly spiral out of control when angry or upset, taking longer to come back down again than the average child. Often sensitively removing them from the situation to give them a chance to settle down without embarrassment or being ridiculed by their peers can help. Once they have calmed down, use it as a learning experience for the child by teaching him how he might either avoid the situation or cope in the future.

Don't engage in confrontations. The child will hold out indefinitely, readily spiral out of control, have the last word and you will always be the loser. Avoid engaging in conflicts over trivial or insignificant misbehaviours or minor rule violations.

MANAGING EMOTION

Music can be very helpful in creating a specific mood and in motivating and getting through transitional times in the classroom. Many children, especially those with ADHD, are able to concentrate and respond better when there is background music. A teacher who is creative will find many ways of using music, both within the curriculum, during transitions and to specifically help individuals with ADHD.

Do not automatically assume that a pupil with ADHD who has headphones on is not doing his work. Some children do focus better when they are listening to music. This needs to be individualized – some pupils will prefer rock music, while most are better with something calmer. However, don't assume that this will definitely work, and try to monitor the child's output during such times. Some children, particularly those who are easily distracted by auditory stimuli, may become worse with music.

If you want to create a calming effect, especially after breaktime and lunchtime, try:

o 'Für Elise' (Ludwig van Beethoven)
o 'Clair de Lune' (Claude Debussy)
o 'Jupiter' from *The Planets* (Gustav Holst)
o 'Nocturne' from *Midsummer Night's Dream* (Felix Mendelssohn)
o 'Humming Chorus' from *Madame Butterfly* (Giacomo Puccini)

For transition times, try:

o 'Pomp and Circumstance' (Edward Elgar)
o 'March of the Toys' (Victor Herbert)
o 'Grand March' from *Aida* (Giuseppe Verdi)

Try to fit the music into the classroom setting. This can be useful for the whole class, but is specifically helpful for children with ADHD.

The continual strains and demands on a child with ADHD at school, the associated underachievement, social skills difficulties and the struggle he faces on a daily basis means that self-esteem and motivation suffer and this can lead to demoralization. Consider whether the child's school environment could be more supportive and nurturing and whether the child is being bullied.

If a child seems sad, miserable and tearful and is despondent within the classroom, it is usually helpful to discuss the situation with the parents, who may need to contact a specialist for advice. Consider whether there are any other issues at school, such as other unidentified learning difficulties, that may be impacting on the situation. If the sadness continues despite supportive therapy then the child's medical practitioner might consider prescribing appropriate medication. Occasionally, manic depression (bipolar disorder) can coexist with ADHD. In the more inattentive-only form of ADHD, which occurs especially in girls, depression is often a coexisting condition.

If the child is on fine-tuned medical treatment, the low mood usually improves. Should the difficulties continue, providing feedback to the child's physician regarding the extent of any residual core ADHD symptoms is very helpful. Adjustments to the medication may be necessary. Communication between the school and the physician is essential. Be aware that medication should not be ceased or dosage changed without reference to the specialist for guidance.

Also consider whether in the educational environment there may be any evidence of autistic spectrum difficulties coexisting with the child's ADHD – difficulty in socializing appropriately, lack of eye contact, lack of empathy, and/or ritualistic or obsessive behaviours. If this is suspected, liaise with the physician and parents.

REFRAMING THE NEGATIVES

The often high energy levels, unconventional thinking and enthusiasm obvious in many pupils with ADHD can also make them uniquely interesting and intriguing to work with. If these attributes can be channelled and encouraged, many people with ADHD have the ability to – and do – become very effective in society and an example to many. However, be aware that some children can feel tortured by their relentlessly difficult symptoms which may not respond totally to medication.

Instead of focusing on the negatives, consider how these can be viewed as strengths and encouraged – for example, a distractible child could be perceived as one who is curious and questioning; those who are impulsive are also often energetic and decisive. If they have the intuition to keep making the correct decisions they can be highly effective in life and often in business or in their career path. Such children can also thrive on tasks that need attention to detail and will perhaps have good debating skills. They may also enjoy being busy and have lots of stamina. They may respond well to having responsibility in groups or tasks. Children who have difficulty in converting words into concepts can be excellent visual thinkers who are imaginative. Speaking quickly often also means thinking fast. Where there is difficulty in following directions, these pupils can be independent, self-motivated and able to use their own initiative.

So, identify the positive attributes of your pupils with ADHD and discuss them with them. Suggest the analogy of a mountain range where there are peaks where they have real skills, and valleys where aspects of their ADHD, such as their weak concentration and organizational problems, hold them back.

Minimize the limitations of their ADHD and play to their strengths as much as possible.

Medication

CREATING A MONITORING TOOLKIT

Educational strategies are always important for children with ADHD, but if they prove insufficient then other strategies, such as medication, might need to be tried. Before the child is started on medication, changes to his diet might be considered. Although these dietary changes have generally been found to be ineffective in improving concentration and impulsiveness, there is a small group of children with ADHD who are particularly sensitive to diet and it may be worth discussing this with the parents.

It is important to recognize that although the decision to treat medically is a joint one between parents and child in conjunction with their specialist, this will invariably have been done after much soul searching. Parents will have had to reach the best decision in the interests of their child. Being part of that decision as a teacher, with an informed, up-to-date, approach to the management of ADHD, and an understanding that medication may have an essential role to play is likely to be beneficial.

It is therefore very helpful for teachers to develop a monitoring toolkit, using a mix of formal and informal measures, and employ these early in their relationship with the pupil. Many physicians will provide schools with a feedback form. It is also worth keeping notes, watching the child's concentration at different times of the day, and establishing a 'baseline' for the pupil's performance and behaviour and how these vary on a daily basis. Each pupil will have times of the day when their performance is better or worse, and if you are aware of this you can significantly help to maximize their achievements.

Research has shown that children with ADHD have differences in their brain chemistry so that their neurotransmitters – the chemical messengers in their brain – are not working properly. This means that thought processes are not transmitted efficiently. The use of medication aims to correct this chemical deficiency and allow concentration and impulse control to work in a more consistent manner.

Try to learn about the various medications that can be used. The development of long-acting preparations has made the management of children with ADHD much easier and more effective during the school day, as a lunchtime dose is often not necessary. They can last for varying periods of time, from 3–4 hours to 10–12 hours. It is therefore very useful for you to understand the duration and action of these preparations, and to find out which one the child is taking.

Be aware of the possible side effects. While there is no evidence of long-term side effects, about 20% of children have experienced some transient short-term side effects including:

○ appetite suppression
○ sleep difficulties
○ blunting of personality.

These can usually be improved or ceased with specialist guidance and careful fine-tuning of dosage.

Make a note of the differences you observe in the child on medication. Observe side effects where evident, but also look for the positives. It may be difficult to decide which issues are part of the child's normal personality and which might be related to medication. If in doubt, or if you are concerned about any side effects, discuss them with the child's parents.

Remember that children with ADHD often respond differently to medication types and dosage. It is a normal part of the treatment process for there to be changes of dose and/or medication. It should be emphasized that this is determined by the clinical judgment of the specialist and the symptoms and associated difficulties of the individual child.

Gifted children with ADHD

RECOGNIZE VARIABILITY

Gifted and talented children without ADHD tend to have a fairly even scatter of abilities. However, those with ADHD can be a challenge to the teacher because of their extreme variability. They have very significant cognitive strengths but may be very poor with social skills, concentration and short-term memory.

Think about how best to handle the gifted child while also supporting his social difficulties. Don't just assume that the child is of average intelligence but think carefully about how he relates to other children in the class in these various areas. This will frequently lead to a realization that the child has a great deal more potential than was previously recognized.

Give the child a task that he perceives as mundane and try to assess how good his ability to concentrate is. Many children with ADHD, especially those who are gifted and talented, have the ability to over-focus on tasks they find interesting, but this can often disguise their difficulties with the mundane tasks and their inability to switch on to them. This 'faulty on-off switch' often seems to be more pronounced in gifted and talented children and thus the diagnosis can often be missed. Don't just assume that because the child is able to concentrate on subject matter that is interesting that he can therefore concentrate on anything at all.

Gifted children with ADHD can become demotivated and suffer from associated problems with planning, organization and time management. Their chronic boredom is a challenge to teachers – average things do not interest them. Acknowledge their need for instant gratification and their craving for a high level of stimulation associated with their ADHD. You may want to get in touch with the National Association for Able Children in Education (www.nace.co.uk).

Gifted and talented children with ADHD usually thrive on complexity. They tend to seek it out, and to seek out peers who have similar interests. Thus it is a good strategy in pre-planning lessons to think of topics or ideas that will challenge the child and give him extra things to think about and problems to tease out. This will help to keep him on task and maintain his motivation.

In the reverse situation, where a gifted and talented child with ADHD is underachieving, it can be a mistake to place him in a lower set. This can exacerbate his demotivation, self-esteem and boredom and start a downward spiral. If this happens then recognition of the child's giftedness is critical, and appropriate classroom support and set placement must be very carefully thought out.

With gifted and talented children especially, the ability to hyper-focus on interesting tasks can often make it appear that the concentration is within the child's own volition. Many of these children have a very strong sense of right and wrong and are clever at practising avoidance strategies. It may not be immediately apparent that they have weak concentration as it may show more as oppositional behaviour or procrastination. Your ability to think laterally and look at things from a different perspective is important here.

If a child has had an educational psychology evaluation done, recognize that even though the test scores are high, in children with associated ADHD they may still be underachieving relative to their innate ability. Some of the tests used are not particularly effective in children with very high IQ, and also the ADHD pupil's problems with poor time management and executive function issues predispose them to underachieve. From the teacher's perspective, therefore, the child may be even brighter than the IQ testing has shown.

Gifted and talented children with ADHD often have very high cognitive ability and advanced needs for complex friendships, wanting to share interests, often related to computers and strategy games. They may have a more sophisticated understanding of the rules and the sort of things they want to do than other children of a similar age. However, their misreading of social cues, their verbal impulsiveness, dogmatism, and difficulty in relating in groups, can often mean that you need to handle them as you would a much younger child.

Because these pupils often seem to be particularly sensitive to minor criticism and appear to be innately aware of their true potential, they often have very poor self-esteem and in the very early years of school can become increasingly demoralized. It's important to nurture their self-esteem, but you will need to find a balance between increasing the level of appropriate academic support and giving support for the social and emotional difficulties.

Be sensitive in reprimanding these children, and aware of their very low boredom threshold and the fact that they frequently see the end result without being bothered with all the boring things in the middle. Such children often have extremely advanced moral reasoning ability and are very concerned about right and wrong and fairness.

Teach specific study and organizational skills. It's often useful to provide a mentor – preferably a slightly older child who has similar interests and can help support them socially and emotionally. These children often know a great deal about a specific subject, but have great difficulty in putting it down on paper in a sequenced and organized way. Here, study skills support, outlining a framework for an essay and praising their positive attributes are essential. Computer work can also be useful, as it enables them to explore topics in more detail. Care, of course, has to be taken regarding excessive internet use to avoid an obsession about computers developing.

It is easy to underestimate the severity of the difficulty ADHD causes in a gifted child because of the masking effect of their intelligence. It is also important not to focus on the disruptive behaviour, but to see the child's underlying high levels of ability.

Parents and colleagues

THERE'S NOTHING WRONG WITH MY CHILD!

Sometimes parents deny or refuse to accept that there is a problem, even though it is very obvious to the teacher. Some may blame the teacher for the child's problems and this can be a difficult situation for you to manage.

Initially it is usually helpful to try to explain to the parents exactly what difficulties you are seeing in the classroom; encourage them to become better informed about ADHD and to ignore the myths which have been so prevalent in the media.

Explain that you believe that the child has potential but is underachieving and/or has behavioural or other difficulties that might be consistent with ADHD. Some parents can be in denial about their child's problem – it is not uncommon to hear fathers say, 'He's just a boy. I was that way when I was his age and I'm OK' – to which it can be helpful to carefully suggest that maybe the child may not be so talented/lucky/have the same issues as the father and that maybe the father's life did not have to be that difficult. Remember that in almost half the cases, the parents may also have ADHD, and about a third of their other children may also have it. It is a strongly inherited condition.

Other parents may have been scared by misleading media reports about ADHD, particularly scaremongering about medication, warned off having their child assessed for special needs difficulties by friends or family, or told they will grow out of it. In those cases it can be a good starting point to suggest some factual reading material for parents and/or suggest contacting a specialist centre for preliminary advice. You may wish to suggest to parents that it is wiser to have a child assessed and receive specialist advice than to leave him to continue to struggle and underachieve educationally.

Suggesting that both parents and school keep a diary of behaviours to monitor the situation together can also be less threatening and help parents come to terms with the situation so that they feel that you are on their side and not blaming them for the child's difficulties. This can be especially helpful where there seems to be a discrepancy between behaviours at home and school. Although there may be several reasons for this, including parenting/teaching styles, school structure/ethos/understanding of special needs, and so on, it does not necessarily negate diagnosis.

THE DISBELIEVING COLLEAGUE

Effective management of a child with ADHD does depend on all teachers having a similar and informed approach to the child. If colleagues are sceptical about ADHD it is helpful to emphasize that it is an internationally recognized, complex neurobiological disorder, affecting up to 5% of UK school children; that researchers believe that people with ADHD have a few structures within the brain that are smaller and that their neurotransmitters – the chemical messengers in the brain – do not work properly, which gives rise to significant difficulties with concentration/hyperactivity/impulse control that can cause educational underachievement. Point out that it is not just a 'North American fad' or a religion to be 'believed' in or not.

Emphasize that although poor parenting or environmental difficulties are often blamed for this behaviour, a child with ADHD is more vulnerable to his environment and that the considerable and challenging pressures of parenting a child with ADHD can cause family dysfunction and tear families apart. ADHD can blight a childhood and damage a future and cause immense stress to the child and family. Understanding the reality of suffering from and living with ADHD is essential to providing the most effective support.

Explain that not all children with ADHD are hyperactive or have sleep difficulties. There are three symptoms of ADHD of which hyperactivity is only one. If it is present, it frequently lessens with time and may no longer be occurring by teenage years, or may be replaced by restlessness of body or mind, or fidgetiness.

And finally, encourage your colleagues to attend in-service training and collect some informed reading material.

Bad behaviour is incredibly wearing for parents and teachers – it's rarely malicious but that doesn't make it any less annoying. It can be extremely unrewarding to parent and teachers alike. Remember that you only have to spend the working shift with the difficult child – parents have to live with him permanently. These difficulties often cause parents to feel very alone.

As mornings are usually particularly difficult for a child with ADHD and his family, with problems and tantrums getting him up, dressed and ready for school, and sometimes school refusal because of the struggles he is having in class, by the time he has arrived at school there may have been a lot of family stress. The child may well be hyped up or upset and need some time to calm down before facing the challenges of the school day.

Don't assume that the problems must be due to inadequate parenting. However, family dysfunction, as a consequence of living with a child with severe ADHD, is often not appreciated and can be seen as the cause of the child's problems. If you are aware of the reality of suffering from and living with ADHD you will be better able to provide effective and sensitive support and understanding to the pupil and parents. Your strategies to help the child will have a much greater chance of success.

Because those with ADHD look no different and have a hidden handicap some people make judgments, such as, 'All he needs is a good hiding/a kick up the pants. I wouldn't let my child behave like that,' without understanding the reality of living with the child.

Don't forget that there are often other children in the family with whom the parents have no such problem. The child with ADHD has been different from the start and stands out as different from siblings and peers at all stages of development.

Recognize that parents often dread going to school in case there has been another disaster – there usually has! – and feel blamed as poor parents and often blame

UNDERSTANDING FAMILIES

themselves. Try to promote a spirit of cooperation and understanding between you and the parents by keeping them informed using regular emails or a home–school diary. You both have the child's best interests at heart and can help each other by sharing information and ideas. Remember, parents usually know their child very well and may well be struggling at home with him as much as you are at school. Ask them which strategies they have found helpful with their child.

It is almost guaranteed that every pupil with ADHD will require a network of support mechanisms to ensure their needs are met. This will tap into a range of 'systems', commonly including education, healthcare, social care and family care. In some cases, forensic/youth justice, mental health, religious and a range of private sector systems or organizations might also be involved.

These systems are often complex and hard to negotiate. Familiarize yourself with key personnel in each area, with the child and parents' consent. Teachers are often best placed to establish links, and other agencies are often keen to hear from them. Such systems may provide you with direct forms of support – for example, someone to share ideas with and to help maintain a consistent and unified approach out of school – or may provide more indirect help such as financial and legal support. It may be necessary to consider whether the pupil will need a statement of special educational needs. By understanding these systems and the role they play, you can become one of the most influential professionals in the pupil's life. It is enormously valuable to such a child to have a teacher in his life who believes in him and empathizes with him, and who understands the often subtle differences in the way he operates. Adults with ADHD often say that they remember one teacher in their school years who really believed in them and supported them and who made all the difference.

It is often useful to identify the best person to support the child's emotional needs. Using a coach or mentor is often very helpful (see Idea 57). This person can be critical in guiding and prompting the pupil to help him overcome some of the difficulties he faces without forgetting the wide range of emotional needs that are likely to need support.

WORKING WITH OTHER SUPPORT SYSTEMS

Transitions

Primary school – usually with just one teacher and being a structured and orderly environment – often provides more stability for the child with ADHD. However, towards the end of primary school, when the work is getting harder, the transition to secondary school can seem quite daunting for these children. The reasons for this include not only the academic work but, in particular, the demands placed on a child in relation to planning, organization and time management.

It is a major challenge for the child with ADHD to be organized enough to get to the right classroom with the right books at the right time. The form tutor or special needs teacher can really help in this situation by working with the child, by looking at his timetable, planning the week and ascertaining exactly which books are necessary on which days, as well as reminding and encouraging him to carry all his books in his bag so that he does not forget them.

These children can also have difficulties adjusting to the change of routine and the change of friendships. A coach or mentor can help to ease these changes and provide support at breaktimes.

It is useful for primary school teachers to liaise with their secondary school colleagues prior to transfer of the child with ADHD. Arrange a meeting or a phone call at the time of the transfer of the child's records. The primary school teacher can then outline the sort of strategies that have been most effective, and highlight the likely areas where difficulties could arise at the new school.

The transition to sixth-form college can be a mixed blessing for students with ADHD. On the one hand they are often getting beyond the broader range of GCSE subjects, some of which were probably not of particular interest to them, and on which they had particular difficulty focusing. At sixth-form college the subjects will, it is hoped, be more to their liking and they will be able to focus better, with fewer problems.

On the other hand, colleges, in their desire to prepare young people for university and adulthood, are less structured and provide less scaffolding than was available at school.

It is helpful for the student's school and college to collaborate so that the most appropriate strategies can be put in place at college. The college day should be structured so that the student is busy for as much time as possible. Clear guidelines and routines are essential.

Computer-based work should be used as much as possible, not only in the classroom but also for homework, as the ADHD student finds it easier to concentrate when using a computer. Students should be able to return homework by email. Planners and diaries are also helpful.

Try to arrange for a regular session to be scheduled with a mentor. This can be another teacher, or particularly a special needs teacher – someone who understand the complexities of teenagers with ADHD. The student can be given help with planning and organization, and have the opportunity to discuss things that are going wrong. Breaking down assignments into smaller, bite-sized chunks is also helpful to an adolescent with ADHD.

It is often at this time that the more impulsive adolescent with ADHD is likely to be easily led by his peers into various misdemeanours. Good role models, involvement in positive activities and careful fine-tuning of medication can be extremely important.

FROM SCHOOL TO SIXTH-FORM COLLEGE

Unfortunately, many adolescents believe that their problems with ADHD are over once they have finished school. Sadly, in many cases this is only the start, and the transition from school to adult relationships and employment can be one of the most testing and problematic times for them.

With the transition to higher education, students with ADHD generally start to specialize even more in their subjects of interest and are therefore able to focus more. However, for many, the prospect of higher education can be quite daunting. The relative lack of scaffolding and structure that is critical for many people with ADHD can be problematic.

University can be quite a challenge. This is especially true if the student is coming from a highly structured school, particularly a private school with small class sizes. Problems are often further exacerbated when the youth is living away from home, often in rented accommodation with other students. Getting organized, paying rent, getting up in the morning, arriving at lectures on time, listening to the lectures and recording them as well as doing essays and revising can all be nightmares for a young person with ADHD.

University tutors need to be aware of the complications of ADHD and that they may involve the frequent pitfalls, such as excessive alcohol or drug intake, impulsive spending, higher risk of unplanned pregnancy and risk of falling foul of authority figures.

Liaison between school/sixth-form college and university, with communication with the university's special needs department, can be very helpful. Such departments are often well funded and may be able to provide mechanical support such as a laptop or dictating system if appropriate, as well as a mentor.

Encouraging the use of a mentor is arguably the most important support for these adolescents. Although most university students have a tutor, the amount of input varies. Having an additional mentor who can aid the student with structure and organization and help him to avoid many of the social pitfalls of university can be extremely useful. It is often at this age that the discrepancies between a student's high academic abilities and his low social skills, organization and other competencies become more apparent.

ADHD
with other
difficulties

Sometimes teachers are in a situation where parents may have pushed hard to gain support for their child, and an understanding of ADHD, yet it appears that the child may be using his ADHD as an excuse. Some children say that they cannot do things because they have ADHD and appear to be using it as a way of opting out of school work or social activities, or have lost their confidence in a situation where the teacher believes that the work or activity could be done.

When this happens it is important initially that you have a good understanding of ADHD and speak to the parents to get their perspective on the situation. If the child is suffering from a lack of confidence, then provide appropriate encouragement and support, and work to nurture his self-esteem. Providing more structure and short-term goals can be helpful.

In situations where the child uses his ADHD as an inappropriate crutch, suggest that the parents revisit the ADHD with the child and explain the issues in an age-appropriate and positive way. There are a number of books written for children with ADHD that are suitable for different ages, from the very young to the adolescents. Having an open and frank discussion with the child can also be helpful as quite often the child may have misconceptions about his ADHD. Situations occur where a child with mild ADHD may equate himself with another child in the class with the same diagnosis but who might be much more disruptive, have a lower IQ, or more social skills problems. In such a situation it is important to emphasize that there are a wide range of different abilities, strengths and weaknesses in children with ADHD, and take care to stress the individual child's strengths.

Most teachers are less willing to make accommodations when they feel the child or parents are taking inappropriate advantage of them. A level playing field is essential. However, do not fall into the trap of necessarily blaming the parents for all the individual child's misdemeanours. In situations where parents focus too much on what the child does not do well, compared to their positives, further discussion may be necessary. If parents are seen to be focusing too much on protecting their child and not pushing him enough or having sufficiently high expectations of him, then again this needs to be addressed.

ADHD AND ADD

Although attention deficit disorder (ADD) is under the broad ADHD umbrella, children with ADD have different problems in the classroom from those with the more hyperactive form of ADHD. This can be confusing for some teachers. Use this list to differentiate between the two conditions.

Children with ADD:

o are usually daydreamers, often 'away with the fairies' in class and therefore not receptive to learning
o are hard to motivate
o are often girls rather than boys
o have never been hyperactive in the past
o are usually not disruptive
o are not easily distracted
o may still be achieving in the classroom, but are underachieving relative to their ability
o may experience other learning difficulties, with mood swings, anxiety or depression
o have brain function problems and so their difficulties with concentration are not of their own volition. Trying to get them to concentrate harder in situations where they are unable to will only have a negative impact on their self-esteem and demotivate them.

These children are sometimes hard to spot as their difficulties may go unnoticed in a large class. So, if you have a child in your class who is persistently daydreaming, consider whether it seems to be beyond the child's control or is within a normal range of difficulties. Strategies outlined in previous pages for children with ADHD generally apply to this group, especially those for improving skills in listening, focusing and concentrating.

Some children with ADHD can also have tics as a complication of their condition. These are rapid, involuntary, recurrent non-rhythmic vocal or motor actions. They frequently fluctuate in intensity, during the day and over weeks and months. Motor tics include recurrent eye blinking, facial grimacing, shoulder shrugging, tongue protrusion, knuckle cracking. They may also be more complex, often involving jumping, lip biting and facial gestures. Vocal tics include throat clearing, coughing, spitting, grunting and whistling, among others.

Some children have severe tics and are diagnosed as having Tourette Syndrome. ADHD and Tourette Syndrome frequently occur together in the same child.

Try to get an idea of the nature of the child's tics and in what situations they are better or worse. You may find that stressful situations, such as exams, can make tics worse. It is worth noting whether the child is able to contain the tics at school, as is often the case. Parents often report that they become worse when the pupil returns home. Ask the child's parents for any suggestions for coping with his tics, as they will almost certainly have found strategies that help.

It is generally best to ignore a child's vocal or motor tics in the classroom and this lead will tend to have a flow-on effect to the other children's attitudes. Ensure that the child is not bullied or teased and that attention is not drawn to the tics by staff or other children.

The child should not be punished or chastised because of them.

If the child is having a difficult period because of the tics, let him take frequent breaks from the classroom to run errands, or find some other reason for him leaving the classroom. This will give him the chance to release his tics.

You could encourage pupils in the class to learn more about tics. Some children with severe tics have given brief presentations to their class on Tourette Syndrome

CHILDREN WITH TICS

and this has subsequently been very beneficial for all involved. However, be very sensitive in suggesting this.

If you need more information on tics, contact the Tourette Syndrome Association (www.tsa.org.uk).

Many children with ADHD also have coexisting features of Asperger's Syndrome or other forms of autistic spectrum disorder.

While some children with severe Asperger's Syndrome or autistic spectrum difficulties are in special schools, there are many other children with milder difficulties who will be found, and cope, in mainstream. Many of these pupils will also have over-focused interests and it is very helpful if teachers and schools can gently develop these in a constructive way. However, such children will often talk about their interests exclusively without recognizing the social skills implications of doing so.

Children with Asperger's Syndrome often find it difficult to cope with sudden changes in routine. They usually benefit from gentle encouragement and forewarning of change where necessary, with the routine being maintained as much as possible in other situations. Understand that if routine is suddenly upset, emotional reactions may occur and it is best to empathize with this rather than punish the child. They often need encouragement with social skills interaction as they tend to be loners and to spend a lot of time in their own company or in solitary pursuits. Help them to mix with other children with similar interests, such as chess, computers or solo sports.

Recognize that these children (and many children with ADHD) are often hypersensitive to many things – ranging from extreme tactile sensitivities where they remove labels from their clothing or prefer certain types of clothing, to an overreaction to certain smells, tastes or food textures. Auditory hypersensitivity may mean that in the classroom they are extremely sensitive to sound, and it is important to be aware of this.

These children often benefit from having specialist support from a regular mentor or nurture group to help with their areas of difficulty, such as making eye contact, taking things too literally, reading facial expressions and emotions, and putting themselves in someone else's

ASPERGER'S SYNDROME (ASD)

141

shoes. Be aware that these pupils may not always pick up on the subtleties of situations and are more prone to being teased or bullied, appearing to be slightly 'off centre'.

Make contact with the National Autistic Society (www.nas.org.uk) for further information.

There is a link between many children who are categorized as having emotional and behavioural difficulties (EBD) and ADHD. Although traditionally there has been the implicit presumption that such children have suffered as a result of their environment, because of parenting, family or environmental difficulties or possibly because of earlier abuse, studies now show that up to 60% of children with EBD also have ADHD, autistic spectrum disorder or related problems.

Children with EBD usually have significant family and social problems. Their parents may be separated, they may live in a poor socio-economic situation, and there may have been issues with child abuse or domestic violence. Such difficulties, however, do not preclude the diagnosis of ADHD, and in fact they are more common in families with children with ADHD.

It is very important to handle these children sensitively and to be aware not only of the ADHD implications, if present, but also of the associated family difficulties, and the social and environmental issues.

Disciplining and chastising these children must be done extremely carefully to avoid exacerbating what is usually already low self-esteem or depression. Such children benefit from tight structure with a delicate balance between clear behaviour management strategies and empathy and emotional warmth.

EMOTIONAL AND
BEHAVIOURAL DIFFICULTIES

Many children with ADHD also have difficulties with speech and language development, and while these are often quite subtle, they can negatively impact on a child's experience in the classroom. One of the most common difficulties is delayed speech, which is more of an issue in nursery and infant school. Children may have either a minimal vocabulary and tend to speak with short, rather immature sentences, or their speech is sometimes unclear.

If you have a child in your class with ADHD who speaks rapidly, mumbles or has indistinct, unclear speech, sit him towards the front of the class and encourage him to speak when spoken to in as clear a way as possible. If the child has problems with sequencing or has a stutter or stammer, try to give as much support as possible and keep him in a situation which is as anxiety-free as possible. Some children show no embarrassment with stuttering but others can become severely uncomfortable, and an understanding, empathetic approach can make all the difference.

The Social Use of Language Programme (SULP) for varying age groups designed by Wendy Rinaldi (www.wendyrinaldi.com) is an excellent way of helping children with significant language difficulties. There are programmes for different age groups, illustrated books with fun characters, and multi-sensory activities to help children overcome difficulties with their listening comprehension. There are also programmes to help children better understand dual messages, multiple meanings and assumed knowledge. If you have an understanding of these subtle difficulties, it is possible to phrase requests and carry out conversations in such a way that the message is clearer, multiple meanings are avoided and no assumptions are made.

The effective use of language can be affected by many ADHD difficulties, including making eye contact, listening, being aware of self and others, interacting appropriately with others without being impulsive, and being aware of the emotions of others. Encourage children to have two-way communication with appropriate listener–speaker exchange. Help them to be aware of their tendency to hog the conversation and not listen, or to continually and impulsively interrupt the other person.

In addition, talk to the child's speech therapist about what other help may be available and whether or not speech and language support in the classroom would be advisable.

Although many youths who have no other difficulties can unfortunately become involved with smoking and excessive drug or alcohol intake, youths with ADHD are at least four times as likely to be involved, and at a younger age. They find that the use of such substances can help them to focus, feel calmer, help with their mood volatility and self-esteem and make them part of a peer group.

Another form of addictive behaviour to which youths with ADHD are more prone is gambling. There is again a very much higher risk to such students because of their need for immediate gratification, with little thought of the consequences. Their involvement with gambling and substance abuse can be due to being easily led, and wanting to be part of a peer group and keep friends.

Adolescents who are abusing substances can create a very difficult situation in the classroom, especially when GCSEs are approaching. If ADHD is effectively managed, when substance misuse is occurring, this usually lessens it significantly. Once medicated, the youth is usually able to concentrate much better, be less impulsive and is able to achieve more effectively at school, with less peer group difficulty.

The teaching strategies for youths with ADHD and substance misuse are much the same as those for any youth with substance misuse. Be on the lookout for:

o dilated pupils
o sudden mood swings
o erratic behaviour – sudden aggression or irritability
o drowsiness in class
o loss of/increase in appetite
o very good and very bad days
o increased defiance.

While these are not definite signs of drug use, they should be noted. Consider being proactive and discuss the situation with the adolescent, linking with Connexions or the local drug action team. Finding a mentor for the youth is often helpful.

Because of their excessive impulsiveness and lack of self-control, some youths with ADHD — diagnosed or otherwise – become involved with the police and other youth justice services while still at school. This is much more likely to happen if the child has been excluded or suspended from school. There is often a history of intimidation or bullying, aggression and disruptive behaviour. Substance misuse may also be involved.

If you are aware of youth justice involvement, an inter-disciplinary liaison meeting could be set up so that information can be shared fully. Consideration of a full assessment through the youth offending team via the Asset mental health screen can be helpful. Work with as many agencies as are available, and be aware of the relevant environmental and socio-economic difficulties. A mentor for the youth is useful here.

It is also often a good idea for Connexions to be involved, and the appropriate youth justice team or drug action team will also have involvement if the matter has come to the attention of the authorities.

YOUTH JUSTICE

As a teacher of a child with ADHD it is easy to get caught up in the daily grind of focusing on all the child's problems, especially when they appear to continue relentlessly day after day. Most children with ADHD are extremely nice children underneath their difficulties, and always have strengths as well as weaknesses.

Try to find these strengths. It may be that they know more about a specific toy, animal or activity than other children and this can be encouraged. Their ability to over-focus on matters they find interesting may lead them to have particular interests which can be built upon to strengthen their self-esteem.

Try to think of the positives as much as possible. For example:

o Hyperactive children can be seen as having high energy, doing lots of things at once, and having the ability to work longer than most other children.
o Daydreaming children can be seen as being imaginative and innovative, as well as creative.
o Daring and impulsive behaviour can be seen as risk-taking or as willingness to try new things.
o Poor planners who are disorganized can also be flexible and ready to change strategy quickly.
o A child who is manipulative might be seen as being a good delegator or able to get others to do things.
o A child who questions authority might be seen as being independent and a free-thinker, able to make decisions.
o A child who is excessively argumentative may be seen as being persuasive or someone who will 'make a good lawyer one day'.
o A child with poor handwriting may 'make a good doctor one day'!
o A child who is bossy and domineering may be a very determined adult and may be good leadership material.
o A child who is strong-willed can be seen as tenacious and able to carry things through.

Teachers often say that the child with significant ADHD in their class is often the hardest to teach and manage. Therefore at the end of the year it is important to reflect on what has gone wrong and what has gone right, to practise forgiveness and to identify the strengths and weaknesses and where things might be improved for the next school year. Being forced to reflect in this way can sometimes shed light on a better way forward, especially when it is done from an understanding of ADHD. Look at which strategies have worked best for the child, whether it has been possible to protect and improve his self-esteem during the year, whether compared to the start of the school year he has matured both in confidence and in his ability to relate to peers. If there are still difficulties in peer relationships, analyse the reasons for this. Is it due to his dogmatism, his impulsiveness, or does he appear to be content without friendships?

Reflect on his academic progress. Is he possibly more talented than has been appreciated? Is he more adept verbally than he is at getting things down in writing, and are sufficient accommodations and supports being given for this? Frequently, problems with written expression mean that these children significantly underachieve.

In so many ways children with ADHD represent one of the biggest challenges for teachers, partly because their very symptoms are the antithesis of what is necessary to cope and achieve well in a classroom setting. On reflection, give yourself credit for all the positive things that have happened and how much progress you have made with the child. Remember to pass on all your knowledge and understanding of your ADHD child to his teacher for the next year.

AND FINALLY...

In reflecting on what has been learned in reading this book, the following could serve as an aide-memoire.

It is vital to understand that ADHD is a neurobiological condition that can lead to significant difficulties throughout life in the basic skills that the rest of us take for granted. Deficits in these areas cause particular problems in the school context.

Environmental strategies to minimize the child's vulnerability are essential. Knowledge of the problems with inattentiveness, self-control and executive functions, and an understanding that while not an excuse, these are outside the child's willpower, mean you are better placed to decide on the appropriate strategies to counteract and minimize the difficulties of the individual child.

Recognize that the use of medication plays an essential role for many children with ADHD, and that it can create a window of opportunity to allow educational strategies to be more effective.

And lastly, don't give up on children with ADHD. They always have strengths, and the challenge is to minimize their difficulties so that they can more effectively utilize these and to help them get through school with their self-esteem, social skills, learning and behaviour abilities as intact as possible, and go on to lead constructive and worthwhile lives.